A Return to Chelm

My Journey to Uncover the Destruction of Two Jewish Families in the Holocaust

ARLENE BLAIER BURROWS

A RETURN TO CHELM
MY JOURNEY TO UNCOVER THE DESTRUCTION OF TWO JEWISH FAMILIES IN THE HOLOCAUST

iUniverse books may be ordered through booksellers or by contacting:

iUniverse
1663 Liberty Drive
Bloomington, IN 47403
www.iuniverse.com
1-800-Authors (1-800-288-4677)

ISBN: 978-1-4917-9279-7 (sc)
ISBN: 978-1-4917-9280-3 (e)

Library of Congress Control Number: 2016904819

Print information available on the last page.

iUniverse rev. date: 3/31/2016

TO THE SPLENDID SIX

Madeleine, Gavin, Payton, Sophie, Sylvia and Mia

Contents

Part One

My brother, David, and I had talked about doing it for years—going to Chelm, where our father was born and our grandfather's family, the Blayers, and our grandmother's family, the Gromans, had lived for generations. Growing up, we heard stories about Chelm, but not many, and all of them scary or sad.

There was the time that the family was visiting friends and lost track of the hour. They found themselves walking home after curfew and had to hide in a cellar. Grandfather Shimon put his hand over the baby's mouth to keep him from crying so the police wouldn't find them. It was a common story heard in many Jewish families. Or the one about my father as a young boy, walking to school past the police station, where there were dogs. The police sicced the dogs on him, which resulted in his only good pair of pants being ripped. Then his father beat him for coming home with torn pants and told him he should walk in a different direction, while his mother assured him she could mend the pants.

Over and over through the years, as we sat down for a lavish holiday dinner in New Jersey, my father would talk about how, as a child, he had once reached for another piece of bread and had his hand slapped because there was not enough bread for anyone to have another slice. At my mother's funeral in 1990, a woman told me she remembered my paternal grandparents from Chelm—Brandla and Shim—and that my grandmother was a very proud woman who

1

kept covered pots of water boiling on the stove so that neighbors who stopped by would think she had food to cook.

There are many other funny or satirical stories about Chelm, a small city in the southeast of Poland. Since the eighteenth century, an imaginary Chelm has become immortalized in Yiddish folklore as the city of wise men or the city of fools by Isaac Bashevis Singer and Sholem Aleichem, among others. When I tell people that I went to Chelm, some are surprised that it is a real place. But a real place it is, in what historian Timothy Snyder has called The Bloodlands—a place that was repeatedly dominated by one power or another, the soil upon which wars were often fought and borders often changed.

By the time I was mature enough, having children of my own, and wanting to know more about the Gromans and Blayers, my grandparents Shimon and Brandla, who in America were called Sam and Bella, were dead. They had left Chelm early in the 1920s, Sam to avoid being conscripted into the Russian army, as "the war after the war" (Poland eventually defeating Russia after WWI to gain her independence) raged on. The conscription was for twenty-five years and was referred to as a death sentence.

How he left Chelm is unclear, although one version is that he and some friends knew someone who could administer drugs that would cause such severe symptoms that he would be rejected for service. He left by himself, leaving Bella with six-year-old Sol (my father), four-year-old David, two-year-old Isadore (Izzy), and six-week-old Ruth. I don't know how he made it to Palestine, but I have been told that he would have had to go to Warsaw to obtain a certificate of entry from the British consulate because Palestine was a British protectorate at that time. There were Zionist organizations in Poland that might have helped him. Izzy reported a memory of his mother crying hysterically and being terrified when Sam left in July 1920.

Six months later, Bella, along with her four young children, said good-bye to her parents, siblings, in-laws, nieces, nephews, lifetime friends, and neighbors and followed her husband. She carried the infant Ruth in her arms and all their travel documents stuffed into the top of her dress. Ruth often reached in and pulled them out, giving Bella extra anxiety. At one point in the journey, they were on a train going through Italy, and when it stopped at a station, a woman gave the children oranges. It was the first orange my father had ever seen or eaten, and he never forgot it.

In 1921, Tel Aviv was a small desert town. The plan was to immigrate to America, which was not possible to do from Chelm, but they believed it could be done from Palestine. Shortly after they all arrived, the quota of emigrants from Palestine was closed, and they remained in Tel Aviv, residing in the Brenner Quarter until 1928, when the door to America reopened.

The Jewish Community of Jaffa and Tel Aviv issued the family a certificate, which said, "MS [the family] had been residing in the country for nearly two years and were well known to their acquaintances as people who have supported themselves from their own labor." It was stamped by the inspector of municipal police.

They had a family photo taken for the certificate. It is the only picture of the parents and their four children that exists. Thus, on October 9, 1922, Sam and his family were granted a provisional certificate of Palestinian citizenship, renouncing their Polish citizenship. Certificate #22261, issued by the order of the British high commissioner, states that Sam was a thirty-two-year-old, five-foot-five-inch Jew from Chelm, Poland, whose wife was Brandel (née Groman) and had four minor children: Shlomo, who was eight years and three months old; Israel David, six years; Izhak, four years; and Esther Rivka, two years old.

Sam was a mason and had worked in Chelm for Bella's father, Chil Groman, who had a masonry business. That's how Sam met and married the boss's daughter. The family story is that Sam built the first brick house in Tel Aviv. That may or may not be accurate, but he did build houses there, including one for his own family. There are photos of him with teams of workers on building sites.

Sam & Bella with from left Izzy, Ruth, David & Sol standing

Construction crew Tel Aviv -Sam back row right with hat

Ruth, who spent the first seven years of her life there, remembers her father returning from work and propping her on the handlebars of his bicycle to ride down to the beach. She remembers the wealthy, friendly Arab family who lived next door in a very large house and how all the children played together. She also remembers her first day of school—which she did not want to attend. Bella walked her there and spent some time talking with the teachers. When Bella returned home, she found Ruth sitting outside the house, waiting for her. This scene was repeated several times until Bella arranged to change Ruth's teacher. All the children learned to speak Hebrew, as Yiddish was discouraged, and Sam learned Hebrew and Arabic in order to do business.

Four kids in sailor suits Bella made

My father, Sol, talked of hunting for snakes with a long, forked stick, as snakes were plentiful. He and his brother, David, were close in age and comradeship. The ten-year-old and the eight-year-old would hunt in the desert, and at night, to avoid the snakes, they would climb up and sleep in the trees. One Friday night in 1926, David fell out of a tree and died the next day. He is buried in Trumpeldor Cemetery, which at the time was far from a populated area and now is in the heart of downtown Tel Aviv.

Sam built a concrete headstone and embedded a photograph of David in it. Sol was sent every day to water the concrete until it set. A devastated Bella insisted upon having another child, and within one year Morris was born. In less than one more year, in 1927, Morris died of pneumonia. Bella insisted this was not "the promised land" for her, and early in 1928, with the quota reopened to the United States, they boarded the ship *Asia* at Jaffa.

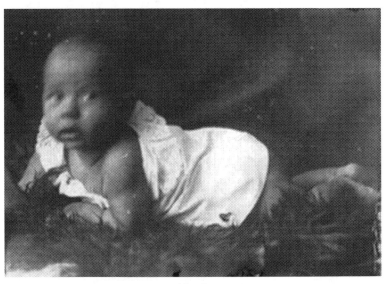

Morris

Like the Blayers, the *Asia* lost her homeland because of World War I, and again like them, she was to have three sequential nationalities: Austria, Brazil, and France (as reparations for the war). She sailed with immigrants between Marseilles and New York via many Mediterranean ports. The ship was small for an ocean liner. It had a capacity of 1,625 passengers (50 first-class, 75 second-class, and 1,500 third-class). The Blayers traveled third class and—at a top speed of fifteen knots—the journey took several months. It was the local, not the express.

Bella packed matzah, as she realized they'd be at sea during Passover, and Sam took advantage of the many stops to visit the ports in Italy. For most of the long journey, third-class passengers were seasick, which left seven-year-old Ruth and nine-year-old Izzy, who were not, free to explore and run around the ship all day long.

The *Asia* landed at Ellis Island in April 1928, but the Blayers were not easily welcomed to America. There was concern that Sam had a communicable disease, possibly leftover effects of the drugs he had taken to avoid conscription, and he was separated from his family and quarantined in the hospital for a week. There's another family tale that Sam's older brother, Uncle Louie, came to Ellis Island and bribed the authorities with a hundred dollars, and the Blayers were released. But this is very unlikely to be true, especially since the notion that Uncle Louie could possibly have had a hundred dollars in 1928—or anytime for years thereafter—is fantastical.

The year 1928 was not an auspicious time to arrive and start from scratch. They went to a flat in the Bronx to stay with the Ledderman family, formerly from Chelm, in their apartment for a few weeks. Another Chelmer family, the Horowitzes, owned a building at 509 Eighteenth Avenue in Newark, and there was an apartment available in that building for thirty dollars a month, so off they went to New Jersey, where they would all remain for the rest of their lives.

As was customary, people from the same towns banded together in the New World and helped each other. There was a Chelmer Society of former residents founded on the Lower East Side of New York City on December 14, 1906, and by the 1940s and '50s, Sam was the treasurer.

When I was a child, they took me with them to meetings, which were conducted in Yiddish. I couldn't understand much of what was said, but did get my cheeks pinched a lot and did understand "shayna maidel," which translates to "pretty girl." They raised money to send back to Chelm and to buy burial plots for themselves. There is a Chelmer Society burial area in the Beth David Cemetery in Elmont, New York. Bella died in 1955 at age sixty-five and Sam in 1960 at age seventy. They are buried there with their fellow Chelmers.

Adapting to a modern American city with a new language was, of course, a challenge. Initially the children attended a Jewish school attached to the Morton Street synagogue. Realizing this was not a good way to help them adapt and learn English, they were quickly transferred to public schools and attended Hebrew school after dismissal.

Although Sol was twelve, he was put at a little desk in the first grade because he did not speak English. As quickly as he learned the language, he was promoted to the next grade, finishing eight grades in a year and a half. Izzy was sent to a school in the Vailsberg section of Newark, which was less urban. It was thought that he might have tuberculosis and the fresh air would be better for him. Ruth's teacher sat her next to Dorothy Kabitsky, a classmate who could translate what the teacher was saying. Ruth learned English quickly.

When 1929 arrived, so did the Great Depression, and so did Leon, the last of the Blayer children. Sam could not find much work, and the family struggled. He did handyman jobs. Neighbors helped each other. Mrs. Minkoff, who lived nearby, had a daughter who owned a bakery. She brought them day-old bread.

Ruth got hand-me-down clothes from the Barron family's daughter. Bella sold her jewelry, including a watch on a long gold chain, which she is wearing in a photo of her taken in Chelm. She also sold a pair of ruby earrings, among other pieces.

Bella in Chelm wearing jewelry

Sol got a job setting pins in a bowling alley after school and worked late into the night to help the family. He would work until three in the morning and then go to school.

The Blayers moved to a smaller apartment at 608 South Twelfth Street, probably because it was cheaper and heat was included in the rent. Six people shared a tiny two-bedroom apartment where you had to walk through the parents' bedroom to get to the back one. The three boys slept in there, and Ruth slept on a cot that was opened each night in the living room. After Sol got married in 1938, Ruth got to join Izzy and Leon in the back bedroom.

Sam was eager to become a US citizen and did so as soon as it was legal, which at the time was five years after arrival. On November

9

19, 1933, Sam and his four minor children became Americans. As part of his naturalization, by decree of the court, his name was officially changed from Shimon to Samuel. Years later, Bella would also become a citizen. On September 1, 1943, at age fifty-four, it was granted and her name was legally changed from Brandel to Bella.

By then I was two years old and had my own name for her. Every time she saw me, her first-born grandchild, she would hug me hard and exclaim in Yiddish, "Gutteniu!" which means "Oh God!" I thought that was her name and called her Grandma Gutteniu for the rest of her life. My parents also referred to her that way, as did my brother born after me. As I now know of the terrible losses she suffered, I understand her cry.

All the children wanted to Americanize their names and changed Blayer to Blaier (pronounced Blair). Ruth inverted Esther Ruth to Ruth Esther Blaier. When she married Ben Berman on April 29, 1944, her initials became REBB, which appear on her car's vanity plates to this day.

Sol, who ran cross country for Newark's Irish American League, gave himself the middle name James—running as Jimmy Blair. He called himself Sol J. Blaier for the rest of his life, even signing his suicide note that way at age eighty-three. Iszak became Isadore but chose to call himself Irving during the late 1930s and early 1940s but after that was always called Izzy.

Sol married Sylvia Kramer on August 28, 1938, and they had two children. I was born on April 16, 1941, and named Arlene Robin Blaier. My Jewish name is Chana Raizel, after Bella's sister Chana and her mother, Raizel, who had died in 1937. My brother, David Lewis (named after David who died in Tel Aviv), arrived on September 11, 1945.

Izzy married Bernice Scheer, who lived upstairs from the Blayers on South Twelfth Street before he left for the army. They were married in the rabbi's house. Izzy had been drafted and was inducted on October 8, 1941, just two months before Pearl Harbor. He served as a medic throughout the North African campaign and then up through Italy. It was a dangerous and emotionally awful job. In 1944, right before D-day, he was in England, getting ready for the invasion, when his commanding officer told him he was discharged and to leave immediately before the base was locked down. The officer had lost all but Izzy and one other soldier in the long campaign and wanted them spared D-day.

One day Ruth and Bella were sitting out on the stoop, when suddenly Izzy appeared, walking toward them. Bella screamed and cried with joy and relief. She had not lost another son. Izzy and Bernice quickly had two children, Herbert David (David after Izzy's brother) in 1945 and Ellen Jane (Chana Sprinzca after two of Bella's sisters) on July 25, 1946. Tragically, Sprinzca had joined the Blayers in Tel Aviv for a short while but hated it there and returned to Chelm, where she was later murdered by the Nazis.

Leon was drafted and served during the Korean War; I wrote him letters several times a month. Sam and Bella endured his deployment by knowing he was a supply sergeant and not on the front lines. His homecoming was a great occasion, with the entire family crammed into Bella's small kitchen. I curled up in a corner on the floor to watch all the joy.

Leon married a woman named Jean after Bella died. Jean was not Jewish, and this was a big problem in the family. At the time, widower Sam had remarried widow Fanny Waldman, who was the mother of Ruth's sister-in-law, Pearl Berman.

Leon did not invite Sam to his church wedding, but Sam was ashamed to tell Fanny that. So he dressed up as if he were going and then called Ruth to see if she was at home. He spent the day hiding in her apartment. Leon and Jean divorced after a few years, and he married Lillian Gibello. They had two sons, Eric on January 19, 1968, and Mark on May 15, 1971.

In the construction boom after World War II, Sam prospered as a mason contractor and built a large brick two-family home in the suburbs for Bella. The kitchen was so big that my mother used to say you needed roller skates to cook in it. Sol, Izzy, and Leon all

11

worked in the construction industry. Sol and Leon supervised the building of large tracts of homes and commercial buildings, while Izzy had his own mason-contracting business.

Ruth worked days as a secretary, putting herself through Rutgers Newark College of Arts and Science nonstop at night and in four and a half years graduated Phi Beta Kappa. She and Ben traveled the world, and she lived in a beautiful apartment filled with lovely furnishings and artwork.

They had all achieved the American dream.

Bella and Sam in 1950s

Bella Blayer died in her sleep on May 12, 1955, at age sixty-five.

Sam Blayer died on November 10, 1960, at age seventy in the hospital after a short illness (probably cancer).

Leon Blaier died on March 2, 1976, at age forty-seven of lung cancer. Izzy Blaier died on September 20, 1976, at age fifty-eight of non-Hodgkin's lymphoma.

Sol J. Blaier took his own life in July 1996 at age eighty-three.

Ruth Esther Blaier Berman is alive and well (age ninety-five) and still driving her Mercedes.

Part Two

*I*n 1986 I saw Claude Landsman's extraordinary nine-hour film, *Shoah*, documenting the Holocaust. The moment that galvanized me was a simple comment: "The trains for Sobibor backed up at Chelm." Sobibor was not a concentration camp but an extermination camp. I remember being told that seventy-two (my brother remembers ninety-two) Blayer and Groman relatives had been murdered in the Holocaust. If Sobibor was so close to Chelm, then maybe that's where they were killed. I wanted to know more about them and about what had happened to them. I have been searching for answers ever since. This is most of what I have found.

Thirty-six thousand people lived in Chelm in 1939 at the start of the war, of whom eighteen thousand were Jews. Approximately three hundred to five hundred Chelm Jews survived the war. Astoundingly, four of them were Groman relatives and four were Blayer relatives. After roughly seven hundred years, the Jewish community of Chelm was extinguished. The details regarding what happened can be found in the Chelm *yizkor* book available online. Yizkor is a Yiddish word meaning a prayer for the dead. Below is a brief summary of those events.

In September 1939, after just nineteen years of independence, Poland was attacked from the west by the Germans and from the east by the Soviets. The Soviet army occupied Chelm on September 14, but in agreement with the German-Soviet pact withdrew from Chelm on October 7 when the German army took over the city.

Several hundred young Jews escaped to the east with the Soviets. Pogroms began immediately, killing scores of Jews. On December 1, eighteen hundred Jewish men between the ages of fifteen and sixty were forced on a death march. Only four hundred survived. All Jews were restricted to a ghetto and subjected to random beatings, killings, and humiliations. Historian Timothy Snyder writes: "in the city of Chelm the robbing of Jews was ordered and women on the street who looked Jewish were stripped-searched and cavity searched. The Nazis broke fingers to get at wedding rings." In May 1941 approximately two thousand Jews from Slovakia were deported to the Chelm ghetto. The first mass deportations from Chelm took place on May 21–23, 1942, when 4,300 Jews including all those from Slovakia were sent to the Sobibor death camp. The final action occurred on November 6, when the entire Jewish population was deported to Sobibor. Only a handful of Jewish workers were left in the town prison to serve the Germans. Almost all Jewish public buildings were destroyed, including the seven-hundred-year-old synagogue. Chelm was liberated by the Soviet army on July 22, 1944.

Six million Jews, one and a half million of them children, were murdered in the Holocaust. The majority did not die in the gas chambers but were shot, burned alive, drowned, beaten to death, starved, or died of disease, like Anne Frank, dying of typhoid fever. Only about two million have been identified. The others will probably never be known, as there are no records of their deaths and no surviving witnesses to tell about them. The Blayer-Groman family is a microcosm of this. I do not know precisely how many were murdered, as I do not even know exactly how many members there were, but I do know about the four Gromans and four Blayers who managed to survive: Gitla Groman Libhaber, her children Simon and Estera Rywka Libhaber, Jankel Burstyn, Naftali Blayer, Chiah Blayer, and Simcha Blayer.

Gitla was Bella's sister, and Jankel was one of Bella's nephews, the son of her sister, Sura. Naftali Blayer was Sam's cousin, who immigrated to Ottawa, Canada, after the war. There were Blayer relatives, Nathan and Ida Blayer, living there who had emigrated from Chelm earlier in the twentieth century. They had changed the spelling of their name to Blair, and he did the same. Naftali worked as a tailor and had a shop in his home. He never had children, as his wife had been used as a sex slave in the camps and was sterile as a result.

Chiah and Simcha were the oldest of the five children of Moshe and Faige Blayer of Chelm and the niece and nephew of Nathan Blair. Nathan was Moshe's brother. Chiah and Simcha were the only survivors of their seven-member family. In Canada, Chiah changed her name to Ellen and married Irving Lithwick. Her brother, Simcha, changed his name to Sam and married Bessie Beckman. After Bessie's death in 1978, he married Anne Ginsberg Mayberger in 1979. Sam and Bessie had a daughter named Ruth who died in 1947 and a daughter named Florence born in 1948 who died in 1968.

Jankel Burstyn was born on January 20, 1916, to Sura Lai Groman and Ruwin Icko Burstyn, a merchant. In 1951 the Blayer family gathered in Bella's kitchen to welcome Jankel (Jack) and his wife, Ernestine, to America. Sam and Bella had sponsored their emigration from the displaced persons' camp in Europe. I watched the joyous event from a corner of the room. They spoke to each other in Yiddish. Ernestine, I remember, had blonde hair. As there was no room in that tiny apartment on South Twelfth Street for two more people, Ruth and Leon went off for three months to Mexico City to live with Bella's brothers, Joe and Izzy Groman, who had left Chelm before the war.

Sam taught Jack how to make challah and found him a job in a bakery. In a short while, Jack and his wife were able to move to a place of their own and open their own bakery in Elizabeth, New Jersey, where they both worked long, hard hours. They had a daughter named Sharon. The business prospered, and Jack used his savings to join with another Polish refugee, Joseph Wilf, a real estate developer. Interestingly, the current generation of the Wilf family are the primary owners of the Minnesota Vikings football team.

Jack became a very rich man, with an office in Bergen County and a large house in Springfield, New Jersey. To this day the Burstyn Group, founded in 1959, develops office buildings and large apartment complexes and is a huge property-management company. Jack died in 1999 at age eighty-three. Sharon Burstyn Green and her husband, Peter, now head the business. During his life, Jack was a philanthropist and on the board of the Rabbinical College of America, whose honorary chairman is Ronald S. Lauder. There is an annual Jack Burstyn Memorial Lecture at Hunter College.

Temple Israel, an orthodox synagogue on the corner of Mountain Avenue and Shunpike Road in Springfield, New Jersey, has Jack (Jacob) Burstyn's name prominently on its facade, as he pledged a large sum of money to have it built. Ironically, it stands facing the Baltusrol Golf Course, which did not admit Jews or blacks until the 1985 US Open was held there and Tiger Woods was to play. Having no way to foresee that Tiger would not make the cut, the club amended its anti-Semitic and racist policy.

There is a photo of a young, handsome Jack standing next to the gravestone of his aunt and Bella's sister, Ita Myrla Groman Tuchsnajder, taken at the Chelm cemetery in the mid-1930s. It was not until David and I were at the Jewish Historical Institute in Warsaw that I learned anything about what had happened to him a few years after that. A pleasant and dedicated woman working in the archives handed me a card that Jack had filled out—a survivor-information record. Twenty-three years old when the Germans invaded, at some point he was sent to Auschwitz, and then in January 1945, as the Germans knew the Soviets were getting closer, they ordered thousands of prisoners on a 276.9-kilometer death march in extreme winter weather with little food, to the subcamp Gross Rosen. Multitudes died during the march; Jack survived. Astonished to be allowed to hold such a document, I ran my finger lightly over his signature, Jankel Burstyn, before photographing the card.

The other three survivors were Bella's younger sister, Gitla, and her two children, Szlama Joel (Simon) and Estera Rywka. Discovering their Holocaust story and finding Gitla's granddaughter, Henrietta, has been a most remarkable part of my search. My aunt Ruth knew that Gitla had married Hersz Libhaber in Chelm and that Gitla, her son, Simon, his wife, Stenia (Stephanie), and their daughter, Henrietta, lived in Melbourne, Australia, but had no knowledge of how or when they got there. Earlier she had maintained contact with her first cousin, Simon, but in recent decades had lost touch. In fact, Simon had come to my wedding in 1963 while he was visiting Groman relatives. He stayed with Jack Burstyn, also his first cousin, who sent a limousine to pick him up when he arrived. Simon also went to Mexico City to see his two uncles, Joseph and Izzy Groman, and their families during that trip. Ruth did not know if he was still alive or how to find him.

Thanks to the Internet, it took less than a day for me to get the information. Ruth knew Henrietta had married Morris Herzfeld and they had two sons, Perry and Andrew Glen. A Google search turned up Perry Herzfeld, a barrister in Melbourne who had argued for marriage equality before the high court. I e-mailed him at his office, and he quickly responded, giving me his mother Henrietta's e-mail address. I wrote to her immediately, and on January 27, 2014, at 6:03 a.m., I received the following:

Dear Arlene,

My name is Henrietta (Libhaber) Herzfeld. I was very excited to receive your email as recently I have started to look into the family history. My father is Simon Libhaber and Gitla Groman was my grandmother. I am the only child of Stenia and Simon Libhaber. I remember that he attended a wedding when he went to America and he always talked very fondly about Ruth. I think he spoke to her on the phone at times over the years.

Gitla and Hersz had three children. Leon, who died as a young child, my father Simon and my auntie Genevieve (Niusha). During the war my father was in a camp in Poland and my grandmother protected him and several other people by sewing clothes for the Nazis' wives. Unfortunately Hersz was murdered by the Nazis by being shot in front of his family. That is why I am called Henrietta which is Henryka in Polish. He died on 6th November and I was born on the same date, but 10 years later. My father and grandmother were released from the camp by the Russians at the end of the war. My auntie Niusha was blond and blue eyed and worked and was part of a Polish family during the war. My auntie, her husband, Fredrick Blondell and their daughter Dianna left Poland illegally and made their way to Australia in 1957. They then organized for my grandmother, father, mother and myself to be sponsored by Jewish Welfare as legal migrants to Melbourne Australia. We arrived here on 25th June 1959.

My grandmother died 17th March 1972. My father is 91 years old and is suffering with vascular dementia. Sometimes he remembers the past, but other times conversation can be difficult.

I have some very old photos of the family. There is one of all the Groman sisters and brothers with my father sitting on my grandmother's knee. He must be about 3 years old. I have other photos from that time and I can scan some in and send them to you.

Going to Chelm should be very interesting and I have tried to look at their records online, but not very successfully. I have much information which I can tell you, but perhaps this is enough for an introduction. It was great to hear from you and I hope you write back soon.

Regards
Henrietta Herzfeld
Melbourne
Australia

Within a few hours, I wrote an extensive e-mail to her, detailing all I had discovered in the past years about the Groman family during my obsessive online genealogical search through Jewish Records Indexing-Poland. I told her that her auntie's name at birth was Estera Rywka. Having to pass as a Polish maid with false papers in order to survive meant changing her clearly Jewish name to Genevieve and using the common Polish nickname, Niusha.

My brother, David, and I had also become active on several Facebook sites dedicated to information about Southeast Poland Jewish Roots; Jewish Ancestry Poland; Jews from Hrubieszou, Chelm, or Zamosc, Poland and had posted the names of our Blayer and Groman family. Exactly one day before I found Henrietta, I received the following e-mail:

Hello, my name is Sharon Groman. I live in Mexico City and looking for information on my ancestors. I found this page of the Jews of Chelm. It caught my attention because it is the only place in which I have seen my last name.

My paternal grandfather came from Chelm and left Poland a few years before the war. He never knew details of his family and not left us much information from his past. For this reason I am writing to see if there is a way to help me get some information about the Groman family of Chelm.

Bingo! I immediately wrote back to her and discovered that her grandfather was Bella's brother, Isak (Izzy). Now there were three Groman granddaughters exchanging information, photos, and getting to know each other.

Dear Arlene and Sharon,

It is fabulous to have this contact with you … I was born on 6th November 1951 in Gdansk, Poland to Simon and Stenia Libhaber. I am an only child. We migrated to Melbourne, Australia and arrived here 25th June 1959. I learnt to speak English and grew up an Aussie child. At university, I studied medicine and still work as a doctor in General Practice. I married Morris Herzfeld in 1978 and we have two sons. Perry is 31 and a barrister and Andrew is 29 and a high school teacher. No grandchildren yet, but I live in hope …

Regards,

Henrietta Herzfeld

The next day brought this from Henrietta:

Simon Libhaber war story

Dear Arlene and Sharon,

Here is a summary of my father's experiences from October, 1939 when the Germans occupied Chelm. He was not allowed to continue high school and had to do labour whenever and wherever the German labour service directed. In 1941 all the Jews were transferred to a ghetto. The labour and abuse continued. The ghetto in Chelm was liquidated on 6th November 1942. On that day Hersz Libhaber was murdered by the S.S. and Gitla, Simon and his sister were taken to a labour camp belonging to the water works in Chelm. Here my father worked in the Gestapo compound while Gitla, who was a dressmaker, sewed clothes for the Nazi wives. The camp was liberated on 22nd July 1944 by the Russians.

A few years ago there was a serial on TV called Blood Upon The Snow. A friend of my father's noticed that in the footage showing the Russians liberating the camps, there was actual footage of my grandmother and father being released. My father did not recognize himself or his mother. I have the footage on tape but find it heartbreaking to watch.

After the war my father was in a sanatorium, and then for a time in the Polish army. He met my mother, Stephania Polawska, and they married. They lived in Gdansk. He went to university and studied commerce and economics and my mother studied medicine and specialised in ophthalmology. I know my father worked for a firm called Chipol Brok, which is still functioning today. It is a Chinese Polish collaborative shipping firm opened in 1951. He worked there as a manager until we left Poland for Australia in 1959.

I do not know many details about these times as my parents did not talk much about their war experiences. When the war was over, my father decided the only thing to do was to lead the best most successful and happy life that he could. Anything less and the Nazis would have won. He could not allow that.

I have only written a summary as the deposition is devastating to read. One day I will share it with you.

I also have a deposition from my grandmother, but it is in Yiddish and only half translated. It seems to be from a book, but I don't know which one. I think my uncle may know. I will get it translated and will share this when available.

On a happier note, prior to our getting in touch, Morry and I had decided that we would do a tour of the US and perhaps Mexico in 2015. It would be great to meet.

Regards,
Henrietta

I immediately went to Amazon and bought the ten-part DVD of *Russia's War: Blood Upon the Snow*, a documentary about the Soviet army during WWII.

I clearly remember as a child in the '40s and '50s that my grandmother, Bella, would telephone my parents and say that she needed to send a package to her sister in Poland. Everyone would contribute. Now I knew who that sister was: Gitla. Henrietta promised to scan and send family photographs. After researching, I had already found the names of our Groman great-grandparents, Chil and Raizla Apelbaum Groman. Henrietta sent a photo of a very handsome man wearing a suit and a tie. After years of searching for Gromans, there he was. It was Chil Groman, Bella and Gitla's father. I posed it on Facebook.

Chil Groman

David and I located Gitla's testimony online in the Chelm yizkor book. It was given on August 25, 1950, in Warsaw. It is not a complete account of all the years of her captivity, and I'm hoping that Henrietta's untranslated Yiddish version is more complete. The testimony is harrowing and a typical example of how the Nazis operated against Jewish populations as part of their political purpose to eliminate the Jews of Europe. Witness testimony of Gitl Libhober (sic) can be found at www. jewishgen.org/yizkor/chelm/Che555.html.

Gitla testified about what had happened to the Jewish community after the Nazis arrived. She names the Nazi officers and tells of the systematic brutality, cruelty, humiliation, starvation, and death they imposed. A smaller portion records her personal experiences.

At the beginning of 1940 we were forced to put white patches with the Mogen Dovid (Star of David) on our right shoulder ... I reported as a foreman and became a dressmaker for the S.D. (Sicherheits Dienst [security service]). Once a member of the S.S., Schteinert, a terrible murderer, and his wife approached me and ordered a dress from me. He demanded that the dress be finished the next morning at 11 o'clock. I answered him that it would be finished at 3 o'clock in the afternoon. After long words, they agreed. The dress was sewn by the morning and I, myself, carried it away. Schteinert met me and asked at what time I was suppose to bring the dress. I answered that I clarified this last night that it could be finished at 3 o'clock and it was now just 2:30. Without saying a word, Schteinert began to hit me, so that I fainted. Then he told the Jews who worked for him that I should be carried to the cellar. When I came to, Schteinert's wife was standing near me and asked how I was doing and said she was delighted with the dress. Agitated, I said: And why did your husband beat me so if this was true? She began to scream that nothing had happened to me and he had beaten me very little and now I should sew three more dresses. When I categorically refused, she threatened that if I did not sew the dresses, she would immediately bring the dogs, which would bite me, and she said that her husband had especially not killed me because my work pleased her and as long as she had me sew dresses I would live. Knowing that I had no other option, I agreed to take on the additional work. My husband was the pharmacist for TOZ (Society for the Protection of Health in the ghetto); my son also worked in the pharmacy. My daughter sewed with me.

Later in her testimony, more mass deportations to Sobibor death camp kept occurring:

November 1942 ... I brought work for the S.D. Horn completely drunk. He then told me that only Jews who were needed tradesmen would remain in Chelm and the rest would be deported. I asked the date, he answered that he did not know exactly. On the 6th of November, Taymer and the S.S. member, Roshendorf, (the worst hangmen over the Chelm Jews), came to the apartments of tradesmen who needed to remain and marked their doors with chalk as signs that they were to remain with the workers and their families. At the same time, they ordered that the doors be bolted and that no one be allowed in. I did what I was ordered to do. In half an hour the S.S. came and took me and everyone, except my husband who had hidden the last moment. My protests and all of my talk about the chalk mark on my door did not help me. I was brought to the square that was on Kopernika Street. On the way the daughter of S.S. Horn saw me. I called to her; she should tell her father that I had been taken. A member of the S.S., hearing my talk, called out to her: Do not say anything to your father. All the Jews must die and at this, Horn's daughter answered: All the Jews can die but not Mrs Libhaber. She must sew my new dresses and she immediately ran away. There were several thousand Jews in the square near the Russian church. The Germans beat them with whips, tortured and bloodied them. The walls of the church were red with blood. Horn came with several S.D. and said I should go with all of mine to the other side where a group of the chosen tradesmen stood. The Jews at the square were ordered to line up in rows of three and they were taken away ... Six thousand Jews were taken then. Many bodies of murdered children and several adults were laid out on the square. The population of Chelm stood on the other side of the church calling out: Good for them; long live Hitler!

The markings on the doors to designate who would be spared death reminds me of the Passover story gone psychotic. Tragically, Hersz Libhaber was not spared. On that November day, he was shot and murdered in front of Gitla and their children.

There is a common belief that because the European Jewish population was destroyed, all traces of them ceased to exist too. This is not true. There are still records of their lives in the archives of the shtetls, villages, and cities where they lived. Sometimes they are incomplete or contain errors of dates or spelling, but they exist. Names are a bit confusing, as each person might have several first names—a Hebrew name, a Yiddish name, a Polish name, and a nickname. There is also a severe limit as to how far back the Ashkenazic Jews of Eastern Europe can be traced, as they were among the last to take surnames. The vast majority did not assume last names until compelled to, beginning with the Austro-Hungarian Empire in 1787 and ending with czarist Russia in 1844. These states wanted the power to directly tax, draft, and educate the Jews, who until then had performed these functions for the state within their own communities.

Until surnames were imposed, names changed with every generation. For example, if Mendel son of Ruven (Mendel ben Ruven) married Ester daughter of Rebecca (Ester bas Rifke) and they had a son named Josef, his name would be Josef ben Mendel.

If a daughter named Sara was born, her name would be Sura bas Ester. Tracing Jewish records prior to surnames is, for all practicable purposes, impossible.

So much of genealogical investigation involves tedious, painstaking searches, obsessively scanning lists relating to births, marriages, deaths, wills, addresses, business directories, legal proceedings, photographs, graves, immigrations, manifests, and on and on ad infinitum—and in this case, often written in Russian, Yiddish, and Polish cursive. Little things I've learned were crucial, such as that the letter j in Polish is our letter y, which meant hunting for Blajer, not Blayer. All the Polish records from 1868 until 1920 are written in Russian.

Stanley Diamond, the head and founder of Jewish Record Indexing—Poland, was a great mentor. I managed to contact him, and we developed a friendly relationship. He taught me many things and even at one point took over my computer to show me how to find the record I wanted. He explained that there are two records for each event: a synagogue record and a civil record, although often the civil record was not recorded until much later or not at all. Many Jews did not report their marriages to civil authorities until the birth of a son, and some civil marriage records include the names of several children—especially daughters—previously born. Some birth records list the child as illegitimate, as the marriage was only a religious one. Deaths were more likely reported to the authorities than births, so at times, most of the children I found for a couple were dead children. Stanley also told me that if I found people with the same surname living in the same area, especially if the surname was not very common, I could assume they were related.

My aunt, Ruth Blaier Berman, was an invaluable source, as her memory is remarkable. My brother, David, also spent many hours on the computer and on the phone with me while we were both searching the same sites. He sent a package of photographs, found when our father died, that were from Chelm. Henrietta and Sharon Groman also sent many photos, and Eric Blaier sent a CD with dozens of family pictures. Many of the photos had no identifying information, and many others did, but it was written in Yiddish cursive, which presented another challenge. I often find myself staring at unidentified photos, as if concentrating on the image will reveal who the person is. Seeing smiling faces dressed in the style of the 1930s still disturbs me; I know what was about to happen to their world and they do not. I want to scream at them, "Run!"

What I've discovered about the members of the Blayer and Groman families is so much more than I ever imagined existed, and the process has been like playing a slot machine. Over and over and over again you get nothing, and every once in a while a hit. Jackpot! The excitement and thrill of each find is exhilarating.

And then there was luck. I awoke on Tuesday, March 4, 2014, to find that Henrietta in Melbourne had e-mailed the many photos she had promised. One of them was very grainy but labeled "Gitla released from prison." Below is the e-mail titled "Watching Gitla" I sent to her, Sharon, and David at a quarter to eleven that night.

I just had the most amazing experience. Henrietta, in one of your early emails you mentioned that there was a Russian made 10 part documentary series called Blood Upon The Snow that had been shown on Australian television and showed Gitla and Simon being freed from captivity. I immediately purchased the DVD from Amazon and Ron and I started watching the episodes last week. This morning I received the photos you sent from your auntie's album including the one of Gitla being released. Perfect timing! Coincidentally, tonight we watched Episode 8, False Dawn, and because I had received that picture, I immediately recognized Gitla and the moment shown in the photo. The narrator describes a prison where only six prisoners have not yet been killed and the film shows them being led out. Gitla is one of the six. In the grainy photo from the album, it is not at all clear what the large figure in front of her is. It is the back of a Soviet soldier in a huge cape being embraced by the male prisoner in front of her and she is reaching out to touch the soldier. I found I was breathless and we watched it in slow motion several times, freezing each frame. I would not have recognized Gitla if only 12 hours earlier I had not received a still photo of that moment. Never did I expect to see my beloved grandmother's sister walking out of prison in Chelm, being freed by the Red Army, on my television screen in Williamsville, New York. For me, that alone makes all the work worth it!

Later on I found out that the male prisoner embracing the soldier is Henrietta's father, Simon.

Gitla released from prison. Simon hugging soldier

On April 18, 2014, Henrietta e-mailed this heart-stopper:

> I found this letter/telegram amongst my father's papers. Since it is in Polish, I can translate it. It is a response to Gitla, who must have written a letter to Brandla telling her that she was alive after the war. I know that there are only a few words written in this, but I feel very emotional about it and can imagine everyone's feelings at the time.
> This is a direct translation. I can read Polish, but it takes me a while.

To Mrs Gitla Libhaber
daughter of Chil Groman
Chelm Lb.
Street Post 39
Newark 11th day October 1945
Dearest Sister,
Your letter of 18th August, year, 1945 arrived. We thank you for it sincerely. We are all well, thank God and we will try in every possible way to help you. Love, kind regards and kisses and we ask to often hear about how you are getting on.
Szymon and Brandla Blajer
608 South 12th Str.
Newark, N.J.

Attached to this e-mail was a scan of the telegram. I've stared at it many times, trying to imagine what this news must have been like for my grandmother. It was right after the war. Did she hope she would soon learn that more of her family had survived—her father, her sisters and their husbands, her brother and his family, her nieces, nephews, cousins, her in-laws? Did she have any sense of the magnitude of her loss? Could she even begin to comprehend that Jewish Chelm had disappeared; that there were and would be no more Gromans in the Lublin District of Poland?

The earliest record of the Gromans in the district is from the shtetl of Siediszcze, which is fifteen miles west-northwest of Chelm. There are records of many Gromans living in this shtetl in the nineteenth century and later, who must be relatives, but I have not yet found many of the links. The names are the same as appear in the next generations of Gromans: Josef, Gitla, Chana, Ita, Szprinca, and Jankel. Although these are not uncommon Jewish names, they are all Gromans. There is a record of a Brandla Groman, married to Szelma Bark, who had a daughter named Malka in 1846. So my grandmother, Brandla, was named after someone on her father's side of the family. Jews name their children after dead relatives, which can serve as an important clue and can also be confusing to the genealogy researcher.

Lejb Ber Groman and Gitla Fajwelson must have been married late in the 1700s, as they had a son—though perhaps not their oldest—in 1801. His name was Josef Groman (died 1876), and he married Chaja Szprinca Drajman (1824–1898), daughter of Abram and Judesa Wajner. After their marriage, Josef and Chaja Szprinca Groman moved from Siedliszcze to Leczna, a shtetl in the Lublin district twenty-nine miles east-southeast of Chelm. These are their children—for whom there are records—who were born there:

- Gitla, 1858 (probably named after Josef's mother; she married Mordke Gersz Berger in 1880)
- Szyja, 1861
- Motel, 1861
- unnamed, 1862–1862 (died)

The couple and their family moved to Chelm in 1862 and had another son:

Chil (Yechiel) Groman 1863–? My great-grandfather!

Chil Groman married Rajzla Apelbaum (1868–1937) in Chelm. Rajzla was the daughter of Szlema Apelbaum (a carpenter) and Estera Rykwa Rajman. This marriage information is indexed in Jewish Record Indexing—Poland and has been a source of much frustration and expense and an example of the kind of problems one encounters. Each marriage is listed in the index with ATKA number, which identifies the record. It is a complicated process to find the actual record using this number. The indexing of the records is done by volunteers who read the record, in this case in Russian, and create a brief description to index it and number that index. Mistakes sometimes happen, as is inevitable.

Raizla and Chil Groman

Using the number on the index for Chil and Raizla's marriage record, I was thrilled to download a copy of the record and found a Russian translator at the nearby university. I sent the record and the money to her and eagerly awaited the translation. I promised David, Sharon, and Henrietta that a surprise was coming. A few weeks later, it arrived in the mail, and the surprise was on me. The document was not Chil and Raizla's marriage but some other couple. One name in the record was Apelbaum, so that may be how the records got mixed up. Never one to accept defeat easily, I asked my contact in Poland to find it for me. He found the same wrong record.

So their marriage record is lost among thousands. But the information on the index that was extracted before the mistake was made states that they were married on June 3, 1896. In 1896, Chil was thirty-three, and Raizla was twenty-eight. Initially it looks like they married much older than was typical at that time. This is an excellent example of another recurrent problem. Their civil marriage was not registered until years after their religious marriage. As explained earlier, this was common. It also explains why many of their children have birthdates earlier than this marriage date.

- Ita Myrla 1888–1933
- Brandla 1889–1955 (my grandmother)
- Gitla 1894–1972 (Henrietta's grandmother)
- Chana Faiga 1895–? (probably Holocaust)
- Sura Lai 1896–? (Jankel Burstyn's mother—Holocaust)
- Szprinca 1898–? (Holocaust)
- Abram Josef 1900–1957
- Brucha female 1/30/1903–? (probably Holocaust)
- Boruch male twin 1/30/1903–12/26/1903
- Icko 1909–1984 (Sharon's grandfather)

That's ten siblings and all I've found. However, Henrietta's father, Simon, said there were eleven, and Sharon reports that her grandfather, Icko, said he had ten siblings, which, counting himself, makes eleven. There's an eight-year gap between Boruch and Icko, so there may have been another child born then. We know that Icko was the youngest child but don't know if Icko and Simon would have counted Boruch, who died in infancy, as one of the siblings. So I am still searching for one or maybe two of Chil and Raizla Groman's children. No records for any births, marriages, or deaths that occurred between 1915 and 1920 exist, as that was during World War I.

Below is the other information I've found about each of these Gromans.

Chil Groman: Hebrew name Yechiel. Sometimes listed as a stonecutter, a bricklayer, or a mason, he was an entrepreneur with a business address at 14 Katowska Street. There is no record of his death, and if he had died before the war, Bella would have received word. Aunt Ruth says she remembers coming home from school and finding her mother crying, having received a letter announcing Chil's death. My notes taken earlier indicate Ruth telling me it was announcing Raizla's 1937 death. A Groman grandchild born to Icko in 1940 was named Yechiel, which would indicate that Chil was known to have died before 1939, by his son living in Mexico, or the child was named after a different deceased Yechiel on the mother's side of her family. There is no death record for Chil Groman in Chelm, but many records are missing. To confuse matters further, on JRI—Poland, I found a page listing survivor proclamations and family searches, and Chil Groman from Chelm is listed. After the war someone was searching for him, to find out if he had survived or where he had died. Others on the page are identified as Town Died: Treblinka or Auschwitz. For Chil Groman, that space is blank.

Raizla Apelbaum Groman: Name is spelled as Epfelbaum or Epelbaum on some records. I was named Raizla after her. She died in 1937. Her birth in 1868 makes her the oldest of her known siblings. They are Mendel Lejbus, born August 16,1877; Joseph, born July 1, 1875; and a sister Golda, unknown birthdate. Golda married Moszek Mordko Szpajzer on February 26, 1896. Moszek's parents were Ajzyk (a locksmith) and Rywka, and they lived in Lublin. Golda moved there, and her children, Aron, born February 1, 1899; Nachman Dawid, born February 17, 1901, died 1902; and daughter Rywka, born April 15, 1905, were all born in Lublin. Daughter Rywka was probably named after one or both of her parents' mothers. There are several other Apelbaums—one named Abram—who owned property in Chelm at 10 and 14 Lacisze Street.

Ita Myrla Groman: Married Srul Wolf Tuchsznajder in Chelm on January 23, 1913, which was the same year her sister, my grandmother Brandla, married on December 26, 1913. Srul's father was Benician from Hrubieszow, and his mother was Estera Miller. There are many Tuchsznajders listed as homeowners in Chelm, including Benician, living at 23 Lwowska Street. There is a family photograph of Jankel Burstyn standing next to his aunt's large gravestone in the Chelm cemetery. Not being able to read the Hebrew inscription, I posted the photo on Facebook, and within fifteen minutes, several people graciously translated it for me: "Here rests my precious and faithful wife and mother Yittah, who died with a good name/reputation on the 27th day of the month of Elul year 5693 at age 44. Yittah Tuchsznajder daughter of Reb Yehiel Groman." The year 5693 equates to 1933.

The inscription indicates she was a mother, but I've never found any birth records. Recently sorting through piles of photos that my father had, I discovered a studio shot of a very handsome young man taken in Warsaw, dated January 16, 1937, and labeled Jacob Tuchsznajder, Ita's son.

Jankel Burstyn at Ita's grave mid 1930s Chelm

Jacob Tuchznajder

Chana Faiga: She is a bit of a mystery, as I have not found any records for her. However, Ruth clearly recalls her mother talking about a sister, Chana, and in a photo of several of the Groman sisters, Simon Libhaber identified one of the women as Chana. My Jewish name is Chana Raizla, and my cousin Ellen's is Chana Sprinzca. Are we named after her?

Sura Lai: Married Ruwin Icko Bursztyn and in 1930 recorded the birth of a son, Szloma, who had been born December 12, 1923. Their only other child I know of is Jankel, the survivor, who was born seven years earlier. It is unlikely that there were no other children born in those seven years.

Szprinca: She is the sister who joined Bella and Sam in Tel Aviv and disliked it so much that she returned to Chelm. There are several studio portrait photographs of her, and she was beautiful. On the back of one photograph, she wrote in Yiddish cursive, "If I were an angel, I would have written to you, not with ink nor pen, only with pure feelings." There is another picture of her handsome husband, Josif Majer Goldhaber, a musician. Their marriage was recorded in 1938, one year before the Germans arrived.

Sprinzca Groman

Abram Josif: I knew him as Uncle Joe from Mexico. In Chelm he worked as a shoemaker at the same business address as his father, Chil. He was married in Chelm to Faige Idessa Rozenknopf—born September 13, 1902—the daughter of Jakob Lejba, a painter, and Szprinca (née Cymerman). Joe and Faige immigrated to Mexico City in 1929 and had a daughter, Lola (Leah); a son, Salo (Solomon); and their youngest daughter, Aida (Ita after Joe's sister). Joe continued in the leather business, and with his brother, Icko, who followed him to Mexico six years later, had a factory that made beautiful leather shoes and purses. Faige ran the retail outlet, and Joe often traveled, aggressively pursuing new customers. They were very successful and even sold their shoes to the Andrew Geller store on Fifth Avenue in New York City.

Ruth Blaier Berman and Leon Blaier traveled by trains from New Jersey to Mexico City, to stay with Joe and Faige. They did so to make room for Jankel and Earnestine Burzstyn, Holocaust refugees, to live with Bella and Sam for three months. Joe took Ruth and Leon with him on some business trips, to show them other parts of Mexico. One night after they all had retired to their rooms, Joe and Leon went out. The next day Ruth learned of this adventure and the reason she was not included. Joe had taken Leon to a whorehouse.

Ninety percent of the time, the visitors lived with Faige's sister, who had a large opulent house and servants. Her husband, Srul, who was considerably older, was often away on business, as he had logging rights in the Tampico Forest. Ruth does not remember the sister's name or their last name but sixty-plus years later remembers that the maid's name was Beatrice. When I asked why this was, Ruth laughed and said that all day long the sister would be yelling "Beatrice," and that was unforgettable. Faige's sister used their stay as an opportunity to travel with them back to the United States, which made that train trip much more comfortable, as she provided a private compartment. After their arrival in New Jersey, Ruth drove her to Philadelphia to stay with friends.

The only time my parents ever took a trip together out of the country was in the late 1950s, to visit my father's uncles in Mexico. My mother returned with a very special gift: a purse made of the skin of an unborn calf. I once borrowed that purse when I was going into New York City on a date. On the long, hot bus ride home and a few too many whiskey sours later, I threw up into the purse and killed it.

There is a zippy film of my parents' visit, most of which was taken by my father. Unfortunately, he had never held a movie camera before and tended to unsteadily pan it at great speed.

When I was seventeen, Joe's daughter Aida (Ita) came to New Jersey and stayed with us. We were about the same age. She wanted to shop for synthetic-fabric shoes and plastic purses to take back to Mexico, as they only had genuine leather there. Aida was clearly not impressed with our working-class suburban neighborhood and expressed her disappointment at the lack of mansions in America. Even more disturbing to her was the fact that my mother cooked, cleaned, and made beds. She had grown up with servants and did not know any mothers who did such work. Later, Aida had one daughter, Dinora Kravetz, and in her twenties and pregnant with her second child, Aida died while on a plane traveling back to Mexico City from a vacation in Acapulco. She had lupus.

Joe's oldest daughter, Lola (Leah), married Enrique Semo, and they had three children: Alberto, who lives in Melbourne, Australia; Ilan; and Alejandro. Joe's son, Salo, married Lily Frimerman, and they had three children and then divorced. Salo was a player, and it is believed that he had other children with other women. Uncle Joe died in his late fifties, and Salo took over the business, mismanaged it, and at one point called Ruth and asked for $50,000—which at the time might as well have been $50 million. Having refused him, she never heard from him again. The business failed. Salo died at age sixty in Israel.

Brucha: Her birth is recorded as January 30, 1903. I've found nothing else about her except that her brother Boruch died on December 26, 1903, at the age of eleven months. So they were twins.

Icko: I knew of him as Uncle Izzy (Isak, Icko) from Mexico City. He is the baby of the Groman family, and his birthdate is recorded in Chelm as December 27, 1909. He left Chelm and joined his brother Joe in Mexico in the 1930s. He became a Mexican citizen in 1940, and on that document his birthdate is December 23, 1910, a year later. Icko's marriage to his childhood sweetheart, Taube Bursztyn, was recorded in Chelm in 1935. Taube, the daughter of

Nuta Bursztyn and Malka Sztiwelman, was born December 5, 1915, which was during WWI and therefore not recorded until 1927. There is a photo of Taube and her sister in Chelm, but no records of this sister or any other siblings have been found. There is another photo of Icko and Taube together in Chelm, with a large gathering of what I assume is the Bursztyn family. As Icko and his sister Sura Lai both married Bursztyns, I initially wondered if they had married siblings, but after further research revealed the Bursztyn parents' names, it is clear this is not true. They most likely married Chelm Bursztyn cousins.

Icko and Taube

While Icko and Joe were building their leather business, Taube bore two sons, Roberto (Ruben) in 1938 and Gil (Yechiel) about 1940. Taube developed cancer and died when her boys were young (about 1948). Through mutual friends, Icko met Marie Share Medwick, a Jewish British woman who was living in Los Angeles, and they married. Marie moved to Mexico to live with Icko and his two sons, and they had three more children.

Saul Groman Share is married to Jane Lupa, a retired schoolteacher, and has three children: Fanny married Amos and has Dalia and Nicole, a baby; Sergio, married to Rita, is an ophthalmologist currently on a fellowship in Denver; and Miriam just married Eddie last summer. Saul is an ophthalmologist and lives in Mexico City.

Icko and Marie's second son, Jaime Groman Share, married Raque Bucay and has two daughters, Sharon Groman Bucay, who found me on the Internet, and her sister, Karen Groman Bucay. Jaime is a dentist.

Icko's youngest child is Ana (Jane), who never married and lives in Cancun.

Icko and Taube's son Gil was run over by a bus and died as a young man. Their other son Roberto (Ruven, Roberto, Robert, Bob) was born in 1938 and died in 2011 after years of battling Hodgkin's lymphoma. He earned a civil engineering degree and then left Mexico to get a master's at the university in Denver, Colorado, where he met and married Debby and had two children: Jeff (Yechiel Josef after his uncle Gil and great uncle Joe) now lives in Chicago, and Tobi (Taube after her grandmother) now lives in Pittsburgh. Jeff is married to Tamara, and they have four-year-old twins, Nina and Jacob, and two-year-old Raina. He is a consultant for a computer-security company, and Tamara is an attorney. Tobi is a pulmonologist, married to Byron Shuman, and they have a son, Eitan.

Icko's granddaughter—and my associate in this endeavor—Sharon Groman Bucay, was born on August 4, 1978, and is married to Mauricio Grinberg; they have two children, Dan age eight and Andrea age six. Sharon studied psychology (it does run in the family) and has a master's degree in family therapy and a private practice.

Her sister, Karen, is three years younger and studied pedagogy.

She is married to Isaac Abadi, and they have three children, Marcos age ten, Esther age six, and Alejandro age three.

After Salo mismanaged the leather factory and it closed, Icko and Marie opened a purse store, and he worked there for the rest of his life. He never talked about Taube, her family in Chelm, his family in Chelm, or what had happened to all of them during the Holocaust. Icko Groman, the youngest of Chil and Raizla Groman's children, died at age seventy-four on July 27, 1984.

Before we leave the Gromans and move on to the Blayers, I should mention Sabina and Eva. I have never found any record of them. They came to my attention when Henrietta sent a studio photograph of her grandmother Gitla surrounded by seven young people. Two of them are Gitla's children, Simon and Nuisha, and her young brothers, Icko and Josef, and there are three other young women. Henrietta assumed they were some of Gitla's sisters. She took the photo with her when visiting her father, Simon, to see if he could identify them. Simon, suffering dementia, easily identified Chana and the other two as Eva and Sabina or as Sabina and Eva; he wasn't sure which was which. Were these the missing Groman siblings? Did Ita modernize her name to Eva? Did Sura modernize her name to Sabina? Or were both or neither siblings?

These are the kinds of questions that plague genealogy research. New findings inevitably lead to more questions. I have recently solved one and a half of these questions. I found a studio photograph of a young woman among my father's photos and had the Yiddish cursive translated: "If I was an angel in the sky, I would have written to you, not with ink and not with a pen, only with pure emotions. Your cousin, Sabina Groman." So Sabina was a Groman cousin, not a sibling, and the quotation on the back of the photo was the same one that Szprinca wrote on the back of *her* photo. Disappointingly, not original and not a glimpse into either women's creativity. This must have been a common Yiddish salutation. I was able to match the face in this photograph to determine which woman was Sabina in the group picture. That left the mysterious Eva. I found an unmarked studio portrait of a somewhat younger woman who looks exactly like a younger image of the Eva in the group photo. She is strikingly pretty, but is she the missing Groman sibling? One common source for answering these kinds of questions is finding the inscriptions on graves and the records kept by cemeteries. For my Chelm ancestors, this is not possible. The cemetery was destroyed by the Nazis, and all the cemetery records were destroyed too.

From left front row - Gitla, Nuisa, Icko, Joe. Back row - Chana, Simon, Eva, Sabina

The Blayer (Blajer) family of Chelm has presented different challenges, as there was no discovered counterpart to Henrietta or Sharon to help me find information. So the majority of what I know has been found in the records. There were more Blayers than Gromans in Chelm, and the earliest record I found is for Mendel and Sura Blajer, who had a son named Michel in 1767 who died in 1832. That would probably put Mendel and Sura's births in the 1740s. I cannot make a direct link to Mendel, but the next-oldest record is a Hersz Lejba Blajer, born in 1815. Like the Gromans and all Jewish families, the names of the Blayers repeat through the generations and are clues, and Lejba is a recurrent name in Blayer families. I believe Hersz Lejba is the older brother of Naftali Blajer (my great-great-grandfather) who married Fajga Rechel (maiden name?). These are the few children I found with direct links to Naftali and Fajga Rechel:

- Srul David, 1848–1916 (my great-grandfather)
- Szandla Ita (female) 1854–1905
- Lejba (male) 1855–?

That's only three children, and it is most likely there were many more children, but the records are extremely sparse. Before I trace the direct line from Srul David to me, I will explain what I learned about his siblings, my great aunt and great uncle.

Szandla Ita: She was married to a baker named Abram Goldman. What follows is a perfect example of how intramarriage was not unusual among Jewish families living in small communities. Szandla and Abram had a son, Naftula Goldman, born October 11, 1876, who grew up and married Fajga Blajer. So both Naftula's mother and wife were Blajers. Naftula Goldman died in 1909 at age thirty-four, four years after his mother, Szandla, who died at age fifty-one. To further exemplify intramarriage, Szandla had a daughter named Maryem Sluwa Goldman, and she married Boruch Nafutla Blajer. Boruch Naftula was born in 1867 to—now get this—Szulim Blajer (died 1898), Szandla's brother or cousin, and—hold on to your hat—Pesia Goldman (1845–1900), Abram's sister or cousin. Boruch Naftula died in 1910, just ten years after his mother, Pesia, at age forty-three. We're not done yet. Abram Goldman's brother or cousin, Jankel Goldman, married Roiza Blajer, and they had a son, Mordko, who died of cholera in 1915 at age thirty.

In the land of the novice genealogist, presenting the above Blajer-Goldman lovefest is the final result of untold hours of frustrating confusion, where bits of information are slowly gathered, mostly from death records where parents of the deceased are listed.

Lejba: Born in 1855, Lejba was a coachman, married to Rywka Listman, and the following are the records I found of their children. Mordko (1883–1895) died at age twelve; Rajzla (1889–1890) died at age one; Naftal (1896–?) and our survivor in Ottawa; Fajga Rechla (?); and Gitla (?). Here again there are more records of deaths than births. I discovered Fajga Rechla and Gitla from their marriage records. It is very unlikely that Lejba and Rywka only had five children, especially as there are so many years between the births.

Their daughter Gitla married a baker named Nuta Diament, registered in 1926, and they had a daughter named Chaja in 1923 and a son named Szolma in 1924. Nuta's parents were Moszek Mordka Diament and Dyna Tenenbaum.

Lejba's daughter, Faiga Rechla, named after Lejba's mother (my great-great-grandmother) married Moszko Truk in 1913. As a reminder, no civil records exist during the First World War in Poland (1914–1920). Children found born to Faiga and Mosko are daughter Hena, born January 13, 1916, and recorded in 1928; daughter Machla, born March 30, 1919, and recorded in 1928; and son Eleazar Ber, born March 10, 1926.

Srul Dawid, (1848–1916 at age sixty-eight "of old age") my great-grandfather, was listed as a worker, a seller, and a stonecutter on various records of his marriage and children's births. As this was not a prosperous Chelm family, Srul probably did whatever work he could find. However, being a stonecutter (mason) continues through subsequent Blayer generations. Srul Dawid married Sura Hartman (1856–1931). Sura's parents were Luzer Mendel Hartman and Estera (maiden name?) from Rudka Opaninia, a village in the administrative district of Chelm. Sura was born there. My great-grandparents, Srul Dawid Blajer and Sura Hartman Blajer, had ten children that I have identified:

Sura Blajer

Abram Hersz, March 5, 1884, a carpenter, married Malia Szyfman and owned property in Chelm at 15a Pierackiego Street and 411 Pieraekiego Street, before the Nazis came. They had a son, Elia Wulf, born November 29, 1904. A daughter, Marya, married Lejba Zelman Stolnik and had two children, Gitla (1925) and Mordechai (1929). Another daughter, Faiga, born August 25, 1918, and registered in 1932, was probably also named after Abram's grandmother. A son, Boruch Hersz, married Marjem Feldmus—registered September 2, 1935—had these known children: Chana, born 1929; Mendel, born 1931; and Meir, born 1938. So as I am typing Meir's birthdate, I start to cry, knowing the Nazis arrived in Poland in 1939.

Ruchla Laja (1886–1912). She had a daughter, Chaya, born in 1910. Ruchla's father, Srul Dawid, testified on the civil birth record that Chaya's father was "unknown." Usually if there was not a civilly recorded marriage, the child's birth record says that the mother is single, and there is a father's name listed, as they were religiously married. So having Srul Dawid testify that his daughter's child has an unknown father is very unusual. It has led me to both romantic and violent speculations. Did Ruchla have a clandestine affair—or worse, was she raped? Ruchla died when Chaya was two, making her an orphan who was probably raised by her extended family.

Luzer Mendel was born March 16, 1888, and named after his mother Sura's father, Luzer Mendel Hartman. My grandfather, Sam, named his youngest son, Leon, Luzer Mendel too, after his mother Sura's father. I knew him as my grandfather's older brother, Uncle Louie, who immigrated to the United States before my grandparents and lived in Brooklyn. He was married to Leah (maiden name unknown), and they had four children. Abraham was the oldest, then came Izzy, Rose, and the youngest, Simon. When Rose married, she moved to Massachusetts. Simon, who was much younger than his siblings, was visiting his sister Rose and went swimming and drowned. Louie was also a member of the Chelmer Society. He appears with my grandparents in a large photograph of the group taken in the 1950s and published in the Chelm yizkor book housed at the New York City Public Library and available online.

Ester was born in 1885 and died May 30, 1889, at age four. I believe my grandfather, Sam, named his only daughter Ester Ruth after this sister, who died one year before he was born. As mentioned earlier, Aunt Ruth reversed her name to Ruth Ester.

Szimon (January 30, 1890–November 10, 1960) was my grandfather Sam. I obtained a scan of his birth and bris record, and here is the translation:

> This took place in the town of Chelm on February 18th 1890 at 9 am. A citizen of the town of Chelm, Srul Dawid Blajer, age 33, a porter, illiterate, appeared in person and in the presence of witnesses, scholars of the town of Chelm, Mayer Shmuel Rosenknopf, age 41 an Moshka Leib Shporer, age 58, presented us a male baby; declaring that he was born in the town of Chelm on January 30th February 11th of 1890 at 6am to his lawfully wedded wife Sura nee Hartman age 33. He did not present his marriage certificate. During the performance of the religious ritual of circumcision the baby was named Shimon. The act was declared, read and signed by witnesses. Rabbi of the town of Chelm- signature. Witnesses - Moshka Leib Shporer, M.S. Rosenknopf-signatures. Keeper of citizens records- signature"

Shimon (Sam) married Brandla (Bella) Groman in 1913. Here is the translation from Russian cursive of their marriage:

> This took place in the city of Chelm on the 26th of December 1913 at 10 am. Announcing that on this date in the presence of witnesses, scholars of

the town of Chelm Mayer Shmuel Rosenknopf age 62 and Abram Shporer age 60 a religious ceremony of matrimony was conducted between bachelor Shimon Blajer age 23, son of Srul Dawid and Sura nee Hartman, born and residing in the town of Chelm, and virgin Brandla Groman age 24, daughter of Chil and Raizl nee Apelbaum, born and residing in the town of Chelm. This marriage was preceded by 3 announcements made in the Jewish Synagogue of Chelm on Saturdays (the 7th, 14th, 21st). Nobody presented objections to this marriage. Newlyweds announced that they did not have a prenuptial agreement. The religious ceremony of matrimony was conducted by Mayer Naigauz in the presence and with consent of Rabbi Joseph Kagan. The document is finished and signed by us and by the witnesses. Rabbi of the town of Chelm - signature. Witnesses - M.S. Rosenknopf and A. Shporer.

Keeper of the records – signature.

I am their oldest grandchild and gave my oldest child, Lisa, the Hebrew name Brandla Shimona in honor of them. Their oldest child was my father. What follows is the translation of my father's birth record:

It came to pass in Chelm on 10 August 1914 roku. It came the resident of the city of Chelm, Shimon Blajer, bricklayer, 24 years old and in the presence of the witnesses szkolniki (teacher, administrator at the synagogue, synagogue members) of the city of Chelm Abram Szpoper, 59, and Mayer Szmuel

Rosenknopf, 63 years old, presented us a child of male gender, who was born in the city of Chelm on the 3rd of August this year at 6pm, born from his wife Brandle nee Groman, 27 years old. After circumcision was given the name Szloma. The act was read and signed.

Obviously Messrs. Szpoper and Rosenknopf had lifetime appointments as witnesses! It also needs to be explained that although the document states in my grandfather's bris record that my great-grandfather, Srul Dawid, was illiterate, that actually means "illiterate in Russian." As explained to me, all Jewish men could read and write Hebrew and probably Yiddish.

When Sam left Chelm in 1920, his father, Srul Dawid, had been dead for four years, but his mother, Sura, was still alive and would be for another eleven years. He temporarily left his young wife and four little children behind. He also left many siblings, their spouses, nieces and nephews, aunts, uncles, and cousins, and a myriad of in-laws and friends. It is difficult to imagine how traumatic such a parting must have been and how desperate and courageous he must have felt to do it.

Gitla (July 2, 1894–1896) died at age two.

Rywka, born September 7, 1896, is a bit of a mystery. Aunt Ruth remembers that her father had a sister whose name she cannot recall. This sister married a man in Chelm whose last name was Saltz, and they immigrated to the United States. They had two sons, whose names she cannot remember, and a daughter named Beatrice. As adults the sons lived in Cleveland, and Ruth went by herself to visit these cousins. Their mother died young, and Mr. Saltz remarried and had two more daughters, Regina and Gladys. Gladys became a chorus girl in New York City, which was both a bit of a scandal and a delight to the family. I have tried to track down the Saltz family but have had no success yet. As Rywka is the only sibling I have no other information about, I assume she is the one who married Mr. Saltz. If not, there is a missing sister.

Jenta (Yenta in English) (?–1994) married Hersz Bichmacher from Wlodawa in Chelm in 1927 and immigrated to Rio de Janeiro, Brazil, before the war. I always knew that my father had an aunt from Chelm living in Rio and that our family used to send her medicine. Ruth and her husband, Ben, had visited the Bichmacher family in Brazil and remembers that Yenta came to New Jersey to visit her brothers, Sam and Louie, and their families. So when I first became interested in learning more about the Blayers, the Rio relatives were the easiest place to begin.

Yenta Blayer

Aunt Ruth gave me the names of Yenta and Hersz's children born in Chelm: their son, Samuel (Srul), born December 17, 1928; and their daughter, Rajzla, born November 5, 1927.

Samuel married Rachel and had two children, Richard and Jane. Rajzla married Helmut Schlesinger and had two sons, Fredy and Silvio.

Aunt Ruth remembered that when she met Jane Bichmacher, Jane was engaged to Isaac Glassman. So in 2007, decades after Ruth's visit to Rio, I googled Jane Bichmacher Glassman, and there she was on my computer screen, wearing sunglasses. There were 374 publications listed for her. She is a sociologist at Rio de Janeiro State University and has a doctorate in Hebrew language and Judaic studies, including such interesting subjects as blacks and Jews and multiethnic issues. At that very time, she was in California, delivering a paper at a conference. I immediately e-mailed her but did not get a response. Several more attempts also failed.

I was discussing this frustration with an acquaintance who is a Jewish woman from Rio, when six degrees of separation emerged. My acquaintance had just returned from a bar mitzvah in Rio for her dear friend's grandson. The friend's daughter, Monica, was married to Richard Bichmacher, and the bar mitzvah boy was Arthur Bichmacher, Yenta's great-grandson! Another triumph for Jewish geography.

Through my acquaintance, I learned that Rajzla Bichmacher Schlesinger, Yenta's daughter, was still living, and I got an address for her. I wrote her a long letter and got no reply. I was informed by my acquaintance that the letter was never received—a common occurrence in Brazil with mail coming from outside the country. So arrangements were made to hand-deliver the letter to someone in Brazil who would then forward it to Rajzla. That worked, and on April 4, 2009, Rajzla wrote:

Dear Arlene,

I just received your message, because Jane (my brother's daughter) was very sick for a long time.
I am very happy to hear from you that your aunt Ruth Blayer Berman is still alive and in good health. [Note: Ruth and Rajzla are first cousins.]

I remember that your father Sol Blayer was the beloved nephew of my mother Yenta.

My husband Helmut Schlesinger died in 1981 and my father Hersz Bichmacher in 1983.

My brother Samuel Bichmacher died in 1993 and my mother Yenta in 1994.

I am 83 years old, I use to work in an Electrical Engineering firm as a bilingual secretary, now I am retired, so I do social voluntary work and I sing in a small choir of elderly ladies.

My oldest son Fredy has a daughter Renata who is 33 years old. My other son Silvio is not married.

Please write and tell me about your family and send me photos.

Hoping to hear from you soon.

Yours sincerely,

Rajzla Schlesinger

The letter came with eight family photos, many of which included Yenta and lots of handsome young people. The photos were carefully labeled, and that's how I learned that Ricardo and Monica have two sons, Arthur and Fabio, and Jane and Isaac Glassman have a son named Rony. I was struck by how much Rajzla and her first cousin, my aunt Ruth, looked alike. I am ashamed to say that I did not write to Rajzla again. I'm not sure why, but it was very complicated getting mail to her, and my life got in the way. I have since tried again to contact Jane Glassman. A woman from Chelm who lives in Brazil and is a Facebook friend knows Jane and was determined to help me contact her, going as far as giving Jane my cell phone number and extracting a promise from Jane that she would call me that very weekend while she was here in the States. She never did.

Raizla Schlesinger in Brazil

Fajga Rechel married Berko Pinkwas Fryd, registered in 1909. Both Srul Dawid and his brother, Lejba, named their daughters in honor of their paternal grandmother. Fajga and Berko's known children are Mordko Pinchos, born November 12, 1899; Ruchla Leja, born June 10, 1901, and died March 17, 1902; Luzer Mendel, born October 10, 1903, and named in honor of Fajga's maternal grandfather; a son named Wiedor, born December 4, 1905; a son named Zyndel, born 1909. Fajga Rechel died in 1925, and Berko died in 1917.

As a side note, there is a Chai Blajer who married Srul Herz Fryd, a mason. They had a son named Mordko Wolf, born April 13, 1903. Both his birth and the birth of Fajga and Berko's son Luzer Mendel were recorded at the same time. Both had sons named

Mordko and husbands named Fryd, and the Fryd and Blajer families worked as masons. Were Fajga and Chai sisters? Cousins? Were Berko and Srul Herz brothers?

I also found a Sura Rywka Blajer, married to Jakob Fryd, whose son Herszko died at sixteen months of age on July 10, 1905. So there are several Blajer/Fryd marriages but no clear links yet. There is a bookkeeper with the last name of Fryd who was murdered on the Chelm death march. It is a hallmark of genealogical research that most findings lead to more questions, endless wondering.

Much of my motivation for doing this research and documentation is to learn about and to remember not just my direct ancestors but also the lost community of Chelm—to name those with whom I probably share a portion of my DNA. Even with just fragments of information gleaned from the records, stories emerge. I found these.

Chana Lai Blajer married Szija Szwarc, and they had a son named Kelman, who died in 1910 at age one.

Ela Blajer married Szejwa Dancygier and owned property at 5 Katowska Street. He was a merchant. In 1939 he registered the birth of their daughter Frajda in 1918, daughter Cypojra in 1921, son Wolf Zelman in 1925, daughter Etla in 1928, and son Uszer-Lemel in 1930.

Tema Blajer married Jankel Zaltreger from Wojslawic and had a son named Towia on May 11, 1904, who died in 1905 at age one. Abram was born in 1909. Mosko, another son, died in 1913 at eighteen months, and Leijba died in 1915 at nine months. I strongly believe that Tema is a close relation, as Ruth remembers her name, but I have not yet found the link.

Icek Blajer married Bajla Glickman in 1827. Bajla's father was Szymon Majer Glickman. Icek's father was Abram Blajer, and his mother was Elka. Icek's brother Mosek died in 1854. Icek and Bajla had a son named Boruch who died in 1831 and another son named Abram Dawid who died in 1837 at age two. Their daughter Masza was born in 1832, married Ezryel Kastenbaum in 1852, and bore Szewa Kastenbaum in 1869. Their son Cypa Blajer (born 1838) married Itta Judessa Blajer. Their daughter Etta died in 1848.

Naftul Blajer married Hena Frydman and owned property at 11 Pilsudski Street. Known children are Srul Lejba born in 1900, Sura Bajla born in 1904, son Szija born in 1907, and son Szapsa born in 1909. Szapsa, a carpenter like his father, married Zlata Niclich in 1935 and on November 11, 1937, had a son Naftul, named in honor of his father. Again I firmly believe this family is a close relation but will keep trying to find the link.

Szmul Blajer married Toba Pijarska, and they had two girls, Gdala in 1926 and Cyrla in 1930.

Samuel Blajer was born in Chelm in 1938.

Srul Blajer married Perla Rosenblatt, and their daughter Miriam was born in 1924, their son Naftula in 1927, and their son Samuel in 1929.

Aron Blajer and Szmul Blajer (brothers?) were both shoemakers in the province of Rejowie. Aron married Ruchla Adler and owned property in Chelm at 11 Sienkiewicz Street. They had Samuel in 1920, daughters Gdala in 1925 and Estera in 1927. Their son Icek died in 1931. Szmul married Tauba Dumkopf, and they had a son named Abram in 1925 and then a daughter named Cyrla, born in 1930 in Chelm.

Fajga Lai Blajer married Boruch Klajner, and in 1899 they had twins, a girl Elka and a boy Boruch. The twins died at age six months.

I also found an index listing the births of some Blajer children born in Chelm the 1930s. Since 90 percent of all Jewish children did not survive the Holocaust, I feel compelled to memorialize them here:

- Gdala Blajer, born 1932
- Abram Blajer, born 1933
- Gdala Blajer, born 1934
- Cyrla Blajer, born 1934
- Etla Blajer, born 1935
- Chaja Blajer, born 1935

- Chana Blajer, born 1937
- Mendel Blajer, born 1937
- Cypojra Blajer, born 1937
- Naftula Blajer, born 1937
- Wolf Zelman Blajer, born 1937
- Heszel Blajer, born 1937
- Lemel Blajer, born 1937
- Meir Blajer, born 1938

Part Three

I purchased our tickets for Poland from LOT Airlines—a website that almost defeated me—nine months prior to our trip, as a birthday gift for David, who was born on September 11, when that date was only special because of his birth. After talking about how we would someday do this, we were finally pregnant.

Stanley Diamond, the head of JRI—Poland, helped me plan a route to get us to all the places David and I wanted to visit. He was adamant that we engage his expert guide, Krzysztof Malczewski, whom we all call Kris. I e-mailed him and made the arrangements, and he sent an itinerary that included all our wishes.

The months leading up to our departure were filled with this genealogy research and attempts to find people to translate the Russian cursive records and the Yiddish cursive written on the back of so many of the photographs I had collected. The Russian translators were easier to get, as I knew a physician who was Russian and willing do one as a favor, but I did not want to impose too much on her. Instead I found a young professor at a nearby university who did translations for extra money and hired her.

Getting the inscriptions on the photos translated was more difficult but ultimately serendipitous. I e-mailed some friends who had been raised in Yiddish-speaking households, to see if they could read the writing, but they couldn't. I posted a few on Facebook and quickly got one translation, but others proved too hard, due to the particular cursive. I saw a small announcement in a local Jewish paper for a Yiddish group that meets once a month at the Jewish Senior Apartments nearby to speak Yiddish. I called the director of the agency, to see if I could bring the photos to their meeting. She encouraged me to come but discouraged me from expecting them to do the translating. She was right. I went to the meeting, where about a dozen seniors sat around a table; several of the women, of course, brought baked goods. We all introduced ourselves with our English and Jewish names, and I found myself among a group of very interesting people, many of whom were well into their nineties and most of whom lived in these subsidized apartments.

To my right was wonderful Leonide, from Belarus, who fought in the Red Army during the war on the China border and was wounded by the Japanese. There were many survivors and lots of *mama-loshen*—mother language, Yiddish itself—which I loved being surrounded by as I had been as a child in my grandparents' homes. They were very interested in my story and my plans to go to Poland, and they asked lots of questions. My favorite one was "How do you know so much about history?" This was not actually easy to answer. They were amazed and excited to learn that records exist of the Jews in who lived in Europe.

One woman spoke no English, so we did not understand each other. At one point she reached out and grabbed my hand and pressed ten dollars into it. I immediately tried to return it to her, but she kept refusing to take it back. Another person watching this explained that I had to take it, as the woman believed I was going to Israel, not Poland, and it was her way of doing a mitzvah—a good deed—to help me with my journey. So with both discomfort and guilt, I accepted the ten dollars from the sweet old woman who lived in subsidized housing. I told them that David and I would be visiting death camps and concentration camps, and if they gave me the names of family members who were murdered, we would say *kaddish*—the prayer for the dead—for them. One woman immediately jumped out of her seat, saying, "I'll be right back," and returned with a printed list of all her destroyed relatives.

Others passed a sheet of paper around and put down the names. They kept thanking me for doing this. But although I had prepared scanned copies of my photos with the Yiddish writing on the back of each, no one could help. They were too old and the cursive too difficult to read.

It was apparent that they loved the meeting as much as I did. I received lots of hugs and good wishes and the greatest compliment when a small group of them approached me and invited me to become a member of the group. I graciously declined but told them I would return after my trip to tell them all about it. We ended with a group photo for the Jewish newspaper, and as I walked out, I delighted in overhearing "Wasn't this a great meeting!" and "Isn't she wonderful!"

But I still had no Yiddish translator, which I mentioned to another friend who was asking about my trip. She thought her brother-in-law could do it and gave me his cell phone number. He was very gracious and told me to send him all the material and to call him when I returned. When I called him, he told me that the writing had been too difficult for him, but he knew a person who could do it and had given it to her. Her name is Leah Greenberg, and she is married to a prominent orthodox rabbi, Herschel Greenberg. In fact, she was both able and very kind to translate all the Yiddish cursive. She invited me to her home and went over each photo and the translation and was just a delightful person. She also interrupted her husband's work so I could meet him, and she invited my husband and me to her house for Shabbat dinner anytime. The flowers I brought her seem insufficient thanks for all she did to help me.

Several difficult things occurred during the months before we left. The most awful was that my first cousin and dear friend, Ellen Blaier Chopp, who had been battling lung cancer, was nearing the end of that struggle. The month before we went to Poland, her granddaughter was bat mitzvah, and I traveled to Miami to attend and to have time with Ellen. She had been involved, wanting to know about the project from the start, and I tried to keep her apprised of each new discovery. She loved the photo of her handsome great-grandfather Chil Groman. She generously gave me an iPad to take with me to Poland.

The hour I got to spend alone with her, listening and talking and letting her cry, was our last time together, and I knew we were saying good-bye, though neither of us used that word. We spoke on the phone a few times after that meeting, and she called to wish me a safe trip. She always did that. I promised to call her as soon as I returned from abroad. I did, but her husband answered her cell phone, as Ellen could no longer speak. She died a few days later. I never got to tell her.

Yom Hashoah—Holocaust Remembrance Day—occurred less than a month before the trip. Some years I attend and some I don't, but I felt compelled to go this time. The memorial ceremony was held at a temple near my home on a Sunday morning. As we entered the sanctuary, we were given a sticky yellow paper Jewish star to wear. I hesitated. All my life, I had been grateful that I was born in New Jersey and not in Chelm in 1941—the year of the Final Solution— and that I had never had to wear the badge the Nazis made all Jews wear under penalty of death. Ambivalently I stuck it on, in solidarity with those we were remembering. Most of the people in attendance were old, which made it clear that as my generation passes, *never forget* will fade away. I realized how deeply I was committed to writing down all I could find out about my murdered family, so my children and grandchildren would know about them.

Each Yom Hashoah has a memorial candle lighting by several individuals in memory of their relatives. Students from the High School of Jewish Studies read the names of victims from *Unto Every Victim There Is a Name* before and after the program. Ironically, the title of this year's program was Children without a Name, which is the story of children in the Netherlands whose parents gave them to non-Jewish families to save them when the children were very, very young. Fifty of these children were captured and went through three camps, Westerbrook, Belsen, and Theresienstadt. They were toddlers in the camps. Forty-nine survived.

Gershom Williger from Canada was one of them, and he was the speaker. He explained the very difficult psychological consequences of living without knowing your surname, your family, your personal history—of having such a void of identity. I have since read many accounts of hidden children and the special struggles they face. In 2015 the Academy Award for best foreign film was given to *Ida*, which is such a story. The program ended with the singing of three songs by all of us: "The Song of the Partisans," "God Bless America," and "Hatikvah."

Our travels had a scrambling start. I was supposed to fly to JFK on JetBlue on Saturday afternoon for our late flight to Poland that night. David would be arriving at JFK earlier on Saturday. Very late Thursday, I got an e-mail from JetBlue with a severe thunderstorm warning for Saturday into JFK, suggesting I rebook my flight at no cost. I hadn't waited all these decades and done all this preparation and research to miss the flight to Poland, so I decided to get to JFK as soon as possible. I rebooked for Friday afternoon, made a reservation at the Holiday Inn Express at JFK, and then was up until two in the morning getting everything packed. I awoke at six.

I hurried to the dentist to get a temporary repair on a tooth that I'd chipped the day before, got my hair blown out, and went to the airport. It took several phone calls to get my boarding pass, as the JetBlue agent who had rebooked my flight over the phone had not completed the task. This did nothing to calm me. The plane was on time, and I sat next to a man wearing a JetBlue uniform. When I told him I was going a day earlier to New York because of the warning I received, he apologized, saying they had a new operations manager who was trying to make his mark.

Retrieving the two suitcases went well, but when I called the hotel to find out where to get their shuttle, I learned that I had to return to the terminal, schlep to the Airtrain, take it to Federal Circle, meet the shuttle there, and then take the very bumpy ride to the hotel. At the time, I thought that was a very bumpy ride, but I had not yet been to rural Poland, where my definition of "very bumpy" changed. The Holiday Inn Express at JFK is on a highway, and there is no place to walk to. I was given a few takeout menus to use to call for pizza delivery if I wanted food. With two hard-to-handle bags, of course, my room was at the end of the hall. But the Wi-Fi worked, and they gave me a bag of trail mix as a welcome gift.

Earlier in the week, I'd received an e-mail from LOT Airlines, inviting me to enter a lottery to upgrade our seats to premium class. There was a minimum offer allowed and then a dial that showed how strong your offer was. I decided to try it, as the flight to Warsaw was going to be a long overnight haul. I was unwilling to put in a really high amount, so I offered a few hundred dollars above minimum, which was rated as a weak offer. I was told I would learn the results the day before the flight. The weak offer won us two upgrades.

My brother, David, arrived at JFK Saturday morning and joined me at the hotel. It had been eight years since we had seen each other, and it was an exciting reunion, mixed in large part with the thrill of realizing our dream was about to become a reality. Our flight was not scheduled to depart until 10:55 p.m., so we stayed in the hotel room as long as possible and then headed for the terminal. The premium-class upgrade meant a very short check-in line, where we got to chat with a Polish diplomat on his way home, who kindly explained why Poland, as a member of the European Union, does not use the euro as currency. I'd share that explanation if I could remember it.

It was disappointing to find out that premium class did not include access to a lounge in which to wait for what was still nine hours until takeoff. David and I both tried pushing that agenda, and the agent suggested we ask at the Lufthansa or South Korean lounges.

Well, the Germans were no help, but that was as it should be, given the nature of our trip. Two old Jews turned away and headed for the Korea Air lounge, where a young woman behind the counter listened to our story about our nine-hour wait and made several phone calls to see if our premium Lot tickets had reciprocity with Korea Air. They did not. We thanked her for her efforts and began to walk away. We got about halfway down a long hall when she came running after us, saying we should go into the lounge but not tell anyone. Eureka! Eight quiet hours on comfortable couches with reliable Wi-Fi, free drinks and snacks, and a big guy with an adorable Chihuahua. Things were turning favorable for us, and that theme continued for the entire trip.

Premium class was luxurious, and the cabin was only about half filled, so before takeoff it was announced that anyone in coach who wanted an upgrade should speak to the flight attendant. Clearly, I could have gotten our upgrades for the minimum price. I don't sleep on planes, even on the longest flights, but with that generous and comfortable seat and an Ambien, I slept for hours.

Arriving at Chopin Airport in Warsaw, baggage retrieval, customs, and exchanging currency all went smoothly. We quickly hired a driver with a large van to take us into the city to our hotel. As he was loading our bags in the rear, David and I went to opposite sides of the van to climb in and simultaneously fell face down onto the van floor. We looked up at each other and laughed hysterically, while the driver quickly ran to me, asking if I needed any help. I assured him that I was fine and that I always fell into vans. He asked if we wanted him to point out the sights as we drove, and he did a good, cheerful job of orienting us.

The hotel was located in what is called the Old City, and that was in fact its geographical location, but old Warsaw is almost nonexistent. It was destroyed and left in ruin by the Nazis. I'd booked the hotel on the recommendation of our guide, Kris, and it was a modern, comfortable, and friendly place. By the time we were in our room, it was midafternoon, and we were eager to get going. I checked the guidebook and realized that we could walk to the Umschlagplatz, which is the site where the Jews were assembled to wait to be transported to their deaths at Treblinka. There is now a memorial there, so we made sure we had our candles and our copies of the kaddish prayer—neither of us know the entire Aramaic by heart—and started to walk down the street.

It was a Sunday afternoon, and the streets were empty until we got closer to the memorial and began to see many young women and men dressed in uniforms. David immediately noticed that they were Israeli Defense Forces (IDF). The memorial is a walled enclosure open to the sky, with a plaque explaining what this place was. On its walls, for the first time, we saw what we would see on memorials throughout Poland. Inscribed were Jewish names—names of men and names of women, but only first names. No one knows what their last names were, but using hundreds of Jewish first names becomes inclusive. We scanned the walls for familiar names and found them.

There were about thirty IDF within the memorial, as David and I tried unsuccessfully to light our candle with matches—our lighter having been confiscated by Homeland Security. An IDF soldier offered us his lighter, and an officer approached and asked if we were going to say kaddish and if we would like them to say it with us. So he ordered the soldiers to surround us, and we all recited the prayer for the dead together. We could not have had a more special or meaningful start to our pilgrimage.

We lingered at the Umschlagplatz for a while by ourselves and then decided to make our way down the street to see the memorial to the Warsaw Ghetto fighters. Along the path we came upon a memorial to Willy Brandt, the German chancellor, who came to the site of the Warsaw Ghetto in 1970, and overcome with emotion, fell to his knees and bowed his head in a spontaneous gesture expressing guilt and asking forgiveness. The likeness of Brandt on his knees is carved into the stone memorial. Years later, he described that moment: "As I stood on the edge of Germany's historical abyss, feeling the burden of millions of murders, I did what people do when words fail." At the time of his gesture, he became a victim of much hatred back in Germany and was denounced as a "traitor of the homeland." Willy Brandt never won an election again.

A short walk through the park took us to the plaza where the memorial to the Warsaw Ghetto fighters towers over the site of the entrance to the former ghetto. As we got closer, there were busloads of IDF entering the plaza too. The granite memorial has two huge menorahs flanking its staircase, which were lit with their flames rising high. There was a platform being erected, microphones being installed, and musicians milling about. Blue and white flower creations in the shape of a Jewish star were laid at the foot of the memorial. David struck up a conversation with an officer, Colonel Gur, who explained that each summer Israel chooses three groups of 188 soldiers from all the IDF units. They are the most outstanding soldiers and are selected to be platoon leaders. Studies show that in twenty years, from the three classes of 188, two of them will be generals. Each group is brought to Poland for a tour of Holocaust sites, to help these young people understand what happened years before they were born and why they must defend Israel's existence.

I told the officer about Gitla, and he was very moved. He told us they would be going to the site where his grandparents were shot. He also was very interested in our story about the Blayers in Tel Aviv in the '20s, but it was obvious that an extensive memorial service was about to begin, so I suggested to David that we move out of the way. The officer asked if we would like to stand with the troops during the ceremony. I said yes, as long as I didn't have to be a reservist. He laughed and directed us to stand front and center of the large semicircle formed facing the monument. The chief rabbi of the Israeli army was there carrying the Torah.

There was a very impressive ceremony conducted all in Hebrew while we stood at attention as instant honorary IDF. Though it is not a language we understand, we well knew what was being commemorated. Kaddish was recited, and the ceremony ended with all of us singing "Hatikvah"—the Israeli national anthem. I stood there thinking about how many of my childhood nightmares had been about being a victim of the Nazis, and now I was a Jew standing on the site of the Warsaw Ghetto, surrounded by a Jewish army, and

I was safe. It was such an emotional and unforgettable experience—almost more than we could comprehend. As we walked back toward the hotel, David said that if we left Poland right then, the whole trip would have already been worth it. I agreed.

Arlene and David with the IDF in Warsaw

Monday, May 12, 2014—There is a new Museum of the History of the Jews in Poland that was open to the public, but its exhibitions were not yet fully installed. The museum sits on the plaza, directly across from the Warsaw Ghetto Fighters Monument, and is a major undertaking of the Polish government to acknowledge the long history and contributions of a people who lived in that country for eight hundred years. Prewar Poland had the largest and most significant Jewish population of any country, numbering 3.5 million when the Nazis invaded. That's why the Germans built most of their death camps there—that's where most of the people they wanted to murder were. The building's entrance is shaped as the Hebrew word *chai*, which means "life."

The interior of the building is architecturally very impressive, and the centerpiece is a replica of a huge wooden synagogue, built exactly as they were constructed for hundreds of years without nails. As timber was plentiful, there were about a thousand wooden synagogues in prewar Poland. They were an iconic part of the landscape. The Nazis burned them, and there are perhaps no more than one or two left in disrepair. The museum chronicles Jewish life in Poland throughout the centuries and had its grand opening a few months after we were there.

Leaving the museum, it was a long walk to the Jewish Historical Institute—in the rain without umbrellas. Finally, according to the map, we were there, but we kept wandering around, trying to find the street. A young student was helpful and showed us the way. We had missed the building several times, as it was tucked away in what looked like a driveway but was a street.

As we bought our admission tickets, I noticed business cards on the front desk with the name Anna Przybyszewska Drozd. I was shocked and excited. That was the person who had graciously translated my father's birth record for me on Facebook. I had assumed she was some generous Russian woman, never knowing that she was the director of the Emanuel Ringelblum Jewish Genealogy Center at the Jewish Historical Institute in Warsaw. And here she was. David and I went to her office to thank her. She was helping a couple from Jersey City find out what had happened to their family. Anna was as delighted to meet us as we were to meet her and promised to help me with more documents. She gave me her e-mail address. That promise has been kept, and we are still in contact. Before we left her office, she insisted on taking a picture of us with the couple from Jersey City to post on her Facebook wall.

The institute houses the Emanuel Ringelblum Collection. Seeing it was close to a sacred experience, both of us had to control our tears many times. As a social scientist, I was amazed at the amount of research and data that Ringelblum's group collected to document everything that was happening to people living in the Warsaw

Ghetto and to people who had been brought into the ghetto from other locations. As a historian, he knew that what was happening to the Jews was unprecedented, and he was determined to record it all. What a masterful sociological project by Ringelblum and the men and women who joined him to do this important work. They called themselves the Oneg Shabbat—Sabbath pleasure—group and met secretly every Saturday afternoon. Knowing that the ghetto was soon to be liquidated, they did two things. They sent every bit of information they had about the deportations and exterminations to the Polish underground, which smuggled it out of the country. And they hid all their materials in three separate caches in different locations. They used large metal milk cans for storage, hoping that someone in the group would survive and return to unearth the archives and let the world know what had happened here.

Two of the Oneg Shabbat group survived and organized the retrieval, but Warsaw was in ruins, and it was very difficult to find any locations among the rubble. Two of the three caches were eventually found, one in 1946 and one in 1950. It is the contents of these that make up this powerful and precious exhibit. Perhaps someday the third one will be found. I encourage anyone reading this to go online to learn more about these people and their extraordinary achievement.

Milk cans

Leaving the archive, we stopped across the street at a KFC to get out of the rain and have cold drinks. Our moods changed, and we walked and laughed, recounting our entrance into the airport van. We got sillier, obviously in reaction to what we had just seen. David told me the story about the name tag he wore at a social event at the international tax attorneys' convention in Paris. Since it's David's life partner who is the attorney, she encouraged him to accompany her. Everyone wore the name of his or her firm on his or her tag. David used the name of a law firm from a Three Stooges movie: Dewey, Cheetum, and Howe. When someone asked which one he was, he answered Cheetum. We were laughing so hard we were doubled over in the rain. There was a couple ahead of us who seemed confused, so we stopped and pointed these people from Baltimore in the right direction. Having been in Warsaw for twenty-four hours, my maven gene had kicked in.

We approached a supermarket and stopped in to explore the wares. It was a very prosperous place with lots of recognizable brands—Tide, Pampers, Lay's paprika-flavored potato chips. We bought some snacks, with lots of help from the woman behind us in the checkout line who understood the Polish coins much better than we did. A glass of wine and hamburgers at the hotel for dinner, and then we went up to the room, where every night of the trip I made notes on the iPad about our day, and we called home for free on the Hangouts app.

Tuesday, May 13, 2014—At end of this day, I wrote, "feels like I'm not up to this task of conveying my experiences here which are so amazing and overwhelming. David could not sleep last night because his head was so full." At eight thirty this morning, our guide, Kris, met us at the hotel, and he was even better than advertised. He is a passionate, professional, knowledgeable, resourceful, dedicated, and delightful man. He began our tour by walking us all around the ghetto area, which is delineated by brass-engraved boundary lines embedded in the pavement. There are many memorials distributed along the route. The Warsaw Ghetto took up 60 percent of the city and was enclosed by a very high brick wall. In order for the gentile population to cross the city, the ghetto was divided into two parts so that one cross street could remain open. A wooden bridge was built over the street to connect the two sides, so residents in the ghetto could get from one side to the other. Much of the gentile population blamed the Jews for this inconvenience. At its height, the ghetto held 320,000 Warsaw Jews and 150,000 Jews from other places. We walked to visit all the memorials to Holocaust heroes.

One was dedicated to Irena Sendler, a Polish woman who smuggled 2,500 Jewish children out of the ghetto. Another was the site of Mila 18, the street address of the headquarters bunker of the ghetto fighters who were led by their young commander, Mordechai Anielewicz. When the Germans came to liquidate the ghetto, they fought back, keeping the Germans out of the ghetto for three weeks. On May 8, 1943, surrounded by Nazis, many died or took their own lives, refusing to be killed by their enemy.

There were hundreds of bunkers built in the ghetto, where Jews hid and fought against capture until the Nazis found and destroyed them all. I had read Leon Uris's book *Mila 18* as a teenager. There is a memorial mound there now with the names of fifty-one Jewish fighters whom historians have identified engraved on it. We placed our stones near a blue-and-white-flowered Jewish star. The IDF had been here.

I won't write about all the memorials, but the one to Adam Czerniakow compels me. In every ghetto the Germans appointed a Judenrat—Jewish Council—responsible for implementing the Nazis' orders. Czerniakow, a Polish Jewish engineer and a senator, was made head of the twenty-four-member Warsaw Judenrat. He worked hard at obtaining exemptions from the Germans to protect the orphans and many others from deportation. When the Judenrat was ordered to round up six thousand people a day, he knew that failure to comply would result in the execution of one hundred hostages. Czerniakow went once again to the Nazis to plead for the orphans. He failed, returned to his office, and took a cyanide pill, leaving a note for his wife: "They demand me to kill children of my nation with my own hands. I have nothing to do but die. I can no longer bear all this. My act will prove to everyone what is the right thing to do."

Other Judenrat heads in other ghettos were not so willing to do the right thing. The most controversial was Chaim Rumkowski of the Lodz Ghetto, the second largest after Warsaw. He was called King Chaim and was certain that his autocratic, slave-driving style and cooperation with the Nazis would ensure his life. He died in the gas chamber at Auschwitz.

It was a long walk with many stops, each with an important commemoration. We saw a statue of the heroic Jan Karski sitting on a chair overlooking the ghetto. Karski, a Catholic military officer, a diplomat, and a spy, grew up in a predominantly Jewish neighborhood in Warsaw. Disguising himself as an Estonian guard, Karski visited Izbica and directly observed what was happening to the Jews awaiting transport to Belzec. He was smuggled into the

Warsaw Ghetto twice to gather evidence, which he passed to the Polish Underground and the Polish government in exile in Britain and the United States government, providing the Allies with the earliest and most accurate report of the mass extermination of the Jews of Germany and Poland.

In 1943 Karski traveled to the United States and personally met with President Franklin Roosevelt in the Oval Office, giving him the first eyewitness account. Roosevelt did not ask anything about the Jews but did inquire about what was happening to the horses.

The full circle found us back at the Umschlagplatz, which this Tuesday morning was rather deserted except for two undistinguished men lingering nearby. Kris pointed them out. They were plainclothes guards. He told us, "Jews are still targets." Next we took a drive to the old Brama Cemetery, which was not destroyed and lies right outside the ghetto boundary. It is vast, 828 acres of crowded tombstones and pathways—a fantastical foreign place. We walked and walked among, along, and between forests of huge headstones, some of which were magnificently carved, and many of which were heartbreaking. Suddenly there was a large open area where the earth was sunken, surrounded by small rocks. It was the site of a mass grave. One hundred thousand people died while being imprisoned inside the ghetto walls. They were carted away to this part of the cemetery and dumped here. The area has become depressed as their bodies decomposed. There were granite caskets nearby marked "SYMBOLIC GRAVES OF HOLOCAUST VICTIMS." David and I placed stones on them, held each other, and said kaddish.

Symbolic Grave

Continuing down the paths, Kris pointed out the bullet holes on many of the gravestones. Part of this cemetery is Catholic, and so during the war, gentiles would come here. Jewish children smuggled themselves out of the ghetto and into the cemetery to beg sympathetic gentiles for food. The Germans would often chase the children and shoot at them. We saw Czerniakow's grave and that of Marek Edelman, a cardiologist and the last survivor of the uprising, who died in 2009.

Walking farther and farther, we approached the huge statue of Januska Korczak carrying and leading a group children. Korczak was a university professor and the director of the Warsaw Jewish Orphanage before the war. In the ghetto, orphans multiplied as parents perished, and the original 125 children grew to 300, as Korczak could never turn any away. Devoted to his children, he confronted the Nazis to provide food for them and was imprisoned and tortured. When released he continued to protect his flock with the aid of Czerniakow. It was when the Judenrat was ordered to deport these three hundred orphans that Czerniakow fatally could not sign that order. Korczak himself could have been spared but refused and accompanied his children onto the cattle car. Keeping them calm, he walked with them into the gas chamber at Treblinka. I had seen a more modern Korczak memorial at Yad Vashem in Israel, and here, as there, I added a stone.

Finally we approached a memorial that was a three-sided structure whose walls were high and built of the same brick as the ghetto walls, topped with barbed wire. The stone floor had a slate menorah image, and in the center was a huge pile of stones. Tucked among the stones were photographs of the smuggler children. It was a tribute in honor of the little smugglers who sneaked out of the ghetto, being small enough to fit through tiny spaces dug in the walls, to find food for their families. There were several plaques on the walls.

One is a poem, "The Little Smuggler."

> Through a hole, through a crack or a cranny
> Starving yet stubborn and canny
> Sneaky and speedy like a cat
> I daily risk my youthful neck
> And if fate will turn against me
> In that game of life and bread
> Do not weep for me, mother,
> do not cry
> Are we not all marked to die?
> Only one worry besets me
> Lying in agony; so nearly dead
> Who'll care for you tomorrow
> Who'll bring you, dear mother,
> a slice of bread?
> Henryka Lazawert
> Ghetto Warsaw 1941

Jack Eisner financed the building of the memorial, and on another plaque is written: *Grandma Masha had 20 grandchildren. Grandma Hana had 11. Only I survived. Jack Eisner.*

Little Smuggler's Monument

As we left the cemetery, we washed our hands—as is Jewish custom—using the old, original water pump.

Kris drove us back to the Jewish Historical Archives, where we had been the day before. He had something special in store for us. We watched a thirty-five-minute film of footage taken in the ghetto, most of it horrendous and some of it Nazi propaganda. Then Kris knocked on a door, and a woman opened it. He greeted her and beckoned us to follow him. Now we were in a series of offices where all survivors' records are kept.

David and I each sat down at a computer and began searching. When we found one we wanted, the wonderfully helpful woman would disappear into the rooms filled with files and bring out the record for us to see, hold, and photograph. We were aghast as she handed them to us—Gitla Libhaber, Simon Libhaber, Jankel Burstyn. It was on Jankel Burstyn's card that we learned that he had been on the death march from Auschwitz to Gross Rosen. They had filled out these documents themselves and signed them. It was as if I were touching their hands.

As we began to leave, the woman started excitedly talking with Kris, and he explained that there was another file pertaining to Simon Libhaber, and she would make a copy for us. After the war, someone had verbally accused Simon of having been a Jewish policeman. This was a transcript of those proceedings and Simon's testimony—a startling treasure.

We drove to a beautiful part of Warsaw where Kris wanted us to have lunch, but all I cared about was his promise to translate these documents while we ate. Nibbling my sandwich with one hand, I carefully wrote each word Kris translated with the other:

There was not ever a written accusation. Someone verbally accused him after the war, and it became a legal matter on January 1, 1946, in Gdansk. He says he vehemently denies it and wants to be exonerated as it "undermines [his] authority and disgraces [his] name." He states that he is not guilty of anything.

Simon Libhaber's Affidavit:

> I was born on March 16, 1922 in Chelm-Lubelski. In October 1939, I hid for three months. In December 1939 I hid with Polish friends from the action. Parents arranged for me to work in the drugstore run by my father, Hersz Libhaber. Then I

delivered letters to people to show up for work and walks to the German office.

In June 1941 Germans attacked Russia. My mother, Gitla, had a shop and she sewed clothes for the Gestapos' wives. During 1941 deportations, I hid with Polish and Ukrainian friends. In 1942, the situation was worse and in November there was the final resettlement and deportation of all Jews except professionals and workers needed in labor camps. Mother got me a job in the labor camp from November 6, 1942 until August 1943. I was sent to work with Sonderkommandos. November 1943 Germans liquidated all Jews and the Gestapo sent me to a jail run by the SS. In jail for three days not knowing what happened to my mother and the rest of the Jews. When released from jail I learned from remaining Jews that my mother stayed alive because Gestapo wives needed her. After that I worked in the field of the jail. In July 1944, the Russians attacked and I was freed from jail. In August 1944, I volunteered for the Polish Army and got a medal. I was in the Army until February 1947 and then lived in Gdansk.

Signature: Simon Libhaber

There is a witness statement supporting Simon's affidavit. The witness is Israel Kupfer. No one in Chelm ever made any charges against him.

Simon Libhaber is exonerated. Not guilty.

I finished my lunch, overwhelmed by all Simon had endured even after the war was over. Then Kris started showing us other parts of Warsaw, including the Panstwowy Teatr Zydowski which is the Yiddish Theater. They were performing a play about Kafka, and as we looked around, Kris began talking to a couple who had stopped to ask him about the place. That's how we met Sam and Lolita. After hearing Sam's story, we invited them to join us for the rest of that day's tour.

Sam was in Warsaw with his Filipina wife, who never uttered a word the entire time we were with them. He spoke Polish with Kris, who translated for us. Sam said he was eighty years old, and he had traveled to Warsaw from Australia to sit on a park bench and die. When he was five years old, in 1939, he was asleep at his grandparents' apartment in Warsaw when he awoke to hear that his parents were escaping to the East and were leaving him with his grandparents until they could return. Sam jumped out of bed and had such a violent temper tantrum that his parents relented and smuggled him out of Poland with them. They fled east to Siberia and then to Uzbekistan. After the war Sam went to the Philippines, where he opened a restaurant and met Lolita, and they ultimately settled in Melbourne.

Now for the first time since he was five years old, Sam had returned to find a park bench to die on, though he knew the one he had sat upon as a child was gone. He told us that his father had been a tailor who made him a magnificent suit of clothes. He had worn the suit to the park and was sitting on a bench when a Polish woman came up to him and admired his clothes. She asked his name, and when he told her, she disgustedly spat and called him a dirty Jew. He wanted to reclaim his right to sit on the bench. His grandfather was a ghetto fighter and organizer, and everyone in his family had been murdered at Treblinka. If not for his temper tantrum, Sam would have been too.

We all walked over to the Nosek Synagogue, the only one left in Warsaw of the two hundred that existed prewar. The Germans used it as a warehouse. It had been beautifully restored by the Lauder Foundation, and there often are not enough Jews for a minyan—ten men needed—to pray. Nearby there is a kosher market.

We all squeezed into Kris's car and drove to a part of Warsaw that is outside the ghetto area and where there are a few prewar buildings standing. We then went to the street that divided the ghetto, where large posts mark the spots where the bridge stood. In all the old photos of Jews crossing the bridge, there is a large building on the corner with a curved facade. I had seen those photos many times, and now here I was, staring at that very building.

Kris escorted us down an alley and into the backyards of houses next to the old ghetto wall. Small sections of the wall still stand, although somewhat shorter, as over the years people have removed bricks to use for their own needs. There were fresh flowers at the base and several plaques attached to the wall.

> In the period from November 15, 1940 to November 20, 1941 this wall marked the limit of The Ghetto. This plaque was affixed by The President of Israel
>
> Chaim Herzog
> during his State Visit to Poland
> May 26, 1992

Another plaque stated, "A casting and two original bricks of this wall to enclose the Warsaw Ghetto were taken to the United States Holocaust Memorial Museum in Washington to give authentic power to its permanent exhibit. August 1989."

Kris drove us back to our hotel, where we said good-bye to Sam and Lolita with hugs. Glasses of wine at the hotel bar helped David and me calm down as we reviewed this extraordinary, emotional day. We would be leaving Warsaw in the morning.

Wednesday, May 14, 2014—Kris arrived at the hotel with his van, which would be our transportation for the rest of the trip. He introduced us to a young man who worked for him and JRI—Poland, who had an assignment to go to a town where they had gotten permission to photograph records so they could be digitized. There is still a lot to be done in Poland, and throughout our journey, Kris would periodically be on his phone, supervising the work. We all got to talk to Stanley Diamond back in Montreal on speakerphone as we drove through the Polish countryside. I'm of a generation that still finds this amazing.

The long drive took us through many small towns, and the farther we got from Warsaw, the more rural the country as highway turned into roadway. Stanley had explained to me months ago that once you get away from Warsaw, the roads are not modern. It takes 50 percent longer to get from point A to point B, and gas is three times as expensive in Poland as at home. I stared continuously out the window, not wanting to miss anything. There still are many small wooden houses built just as they have been for centuries and many large stork nests built atop telephone poles.

Kris suggested we stop to get something for a snack, as we had a long ride ahead of us, and he pulled over in front of a small bakery with a colorful awning. The bakery produced only bread and rolls and smelled wonderful. Kris bought himself a couple of rolls. I was startled to see loaves of challah piled up and eagerly purchased one. Challah, the traditional Sabbath bread, is still baked daily in Poland by gentiles who do not think of it as Jewish but as a bread that has been incorporated into their culture after hundreds of years of being exposed to it. We returned to the van and it wasn't long before David and I were tearing that challah apart and devouring it. It was sweeter than what we're used to, but we sure enjoyed it.

We stopped in the village of Radzymia to visit the small house where Nobel Laureate Isaac Bashevis Singer grew up. I felt regretful that my husband, Ron, was not here, as he has collected and read all of Singer's voluminous work. Then it was on to Wyszkow to see a memorial to Mordicah Androwich, leader of the Warsaw Ghetto uprising, built on the site where his family home once stood. We were driving northeast from Warsaw, and the towns and villages were not prosperous places. We were making our way to Treblinka.

Treblinka was one of three secret extermination camps, the other two being Belzec and Sobibor, which were built in remote areas where the Nazis tried to hide what they were doing. We were the only people there when we pulled into the parking lot and purchased our entrance tickets. Then we began the long walk into the site of the extermination camp where 700,000 to 900,000 Jews and 2,000 Romani were killed; more than any other camp apart from Auschwitz.

At extermination camps people went directly from the trains to the gas chamber. The only stops along the way were to have your head shaved, to have your possessions confiscated, and to be stripped naked, under the false pretense of going to get a shower, only to be herded roughly down a narrow passage which the Nazis called "the road to heaven" into the gas chamber. A small number of men who were not killed immediately were used as Sonderkommandos, forced slave labor, whose jobs were to bury the bodies in the mass graves they had to dig. In August 1943 the Sonderkommandos revolted, killing several SS guards. Two hundred prisoners escaped, of whom nearly one hundred survived the pursuit. By October 1943 gassing operations at Treblinka ended, and the camp was dismantled to hide any evidence of the genocide as the Soviet army was getting closer.

There is a large stone archway as you enter the site and then a long row of concrete blocks shaped like railroad ties to mark the former rail line into the camp. Reaching the end of the line, turning left, there is a huge carved stone memorial towering over a vast, open area covered with 1,700 various-sized jagged, white granite stones. It is a symbolic cemetery. Each stone has the name of a place from which its Jews were taken to be murdered here. The enormous number of these markers surrounding us on all sides was overwhelming.

We lit our candle and said kaddish, adding the names of the people we had collected, who had perished at Treblinka, in front of the huge stone memorial. Nearby was another blue-and-white-flowered Jewish star. The IDF were still ahead of us. David and I wandered around the field of granite markers, randomly placing stones atop them. We came across a worker engraving the name of another town, Blizyn, into one of the markers and then blackening the letters, as they are on each stone. The mayor of Blizyn had recently decided to provide the funds for this memorial.

A man I met on Facebook asked me to place a stone for him on the marker for the town of Locise. I found it, did so, and took a picture to send him. On the edge of the field are some signs and photos briefly describing the history and showing the Nazis in charge. Slowly, silently, and separately we made our way out of the camp, over its uneven ground. It was a beautiful, warm, sunny day, and the camp was set within a lush, green forest. We heard the constant sound of birdsong. It was all so beautiful and such a disorienting contrast.

Treblinka

Back in the van we went and on to more bumpy roads through the dark forest. We stopped at a larger town, Radzyn Podlaski, for lunch at a rather fancy restaurant in what once must have been the home of a wealthy family. Kris had a surprise for us, having arranged for the town's pastor—Tomasz Manko, a Protestant Evangelical minister—to join us. Tomasz spoke only Polish, so Kris had to eat and translate simultaneously. Tomasz explained that at his initiative, the town has repented for what had happened to its six thousand Jews and that currently they were sheltering forty Jewish refugees who had just fled the crisis in Ukraine.

After lunch we began our long drive to Wlodawa, which would take up the rest of the afternoon, and where we would spend the night. Stanley had told me that hotels in the big cities were comparable in quality and price to Western European hotels, but once we were in rural Poland, both price and quality would descend. He was right, but we didn't care. As someone who had slept on a sandy stone floor in a Tel Aviv youth hostel fifty years ago, anything above that baseline is acceptable.

The long drive afforded quiet time not just to think but to feel, and I felt a connection with this landscape, with being a Jew, with what is called one's roots, a homecoming. I wasn't thinking about it; I was experiencing it. In some strange way, I felt like I belonged here, as if my DNA had memory. The feeling was so powerful, I quietly cried.

Thursday, May 15, 2014—Wlodawa is a charming old town with a central square. It is much as it was prewar. Kris introduced us to another Kris—Kris 2—who would accompany us on our tour. Kris 2 was a man of little means, disliked by some in this town where he was born because of his devotion to remembering the Jews of Wlodawa. They were 60 percent of the population (6,000) when the Nazis invaded. His family had many Jewish friends, and as a very young boy, so did he. He had made it his job to commemorate the lost Jews.

There were three religions practiced in Wlodawa before the war, and so there are two churches and two synagogues still there. Our first visit was to the Slavic Orthodox Church, where an inhospitable woman reluctantly got the key to let us in. The place was cavernous, dark, cold, and a bit creepy. I, who am obsessed with architecture, was eager to get out of there. Behind the church there is a wall, and we peered over it to see the Bug River and Belarus on the opposite shore. That land used to be part of Poland, and the Wlodawa train station was there, but after the war, the Soviets moved the border, and it is now Belarus. Kris 2 has a visa which allows him to cross the border, and he regularly wanders Belarus to find abandoned Jewish cemeteries, photographs the headstones, and posts the photos online.

We walked through the quaint town up the hill to visit the beautiful Catholic church, passing along the way a cobblestone street that led down to the river. This is the street the Jews were herded down, from the stadium where they were held, on their way across the river to the train station for their final journey to Sobibor. Inside the church is a memorial to parishioners who were killed.

Kris 2 explained that there was a "good Nazi" named Falkenberg who was in charge of a project to drain a large pond and selected two hundred Jews to do the work. He treated them well, and most of them survived. Today there are no Jews in Wlodawa—well, perhaps a half a Jew—and we proceeded to her ice-cream shop. Mrs. Hirsch is a sixty-two-year-old woman whose father was Jewish. She was excited to meet us and eagerly shared the photo album of her trip to Israel. She phoned her husband so that he could meet us too. She was delightful.

We made our way toward the two synagogues, passing an impressive memorial to the partisans who fought against the Soviet takeover after the Germans were defeated. Along the streets are murals with Jewish motifs on the town's buildings and large blown-up photographs of Jewish life before the Nazis came. Kris 2 has erected all this, and he produces the Festival of Three Cultures every year. He is proudest of the work he has done to help restore the complex of synagogue buildings in Wlodawa.

The Great Synagogue was erected in 1764–1774 in the baroque style and indeed is magnificent, having been restored since the Nazis and Soviets used it as a warehouse and stables. It is now a museum, exhibiting the history of Jews of Wlodawa and much Judaica excavated from Jewish neighborhoods, donated or purchased from antique shops and private collectors throughout Poland. It was here, for the first of what would be many times, that I painfully felt the absence of the vanished civilization of the Polish Jews. I found myself thinking of my visit to the Mayan pyramids and other museums housing the artifacts of former peoples and knew that's what we were doing here—visiting the relics of an extinct culture. The smaller second synagogue is only partly restored, as its benefactor died before the work was finished. On the grounds is a large rock with a plaque that Kris 2 was instrumental in obtaining and proudly showed us. It reads in Polish and English: IN MEMORY OF THE JEWS OF WLODAWA.

We took Kris 2 with us for a really delicious lunch, our first excellent Polish meal. We then drove to the Bug River, the same river that divides Chelm, and hiked down a dirt path to look across to Belarus. The border is marked by a few red-and-white-striped poles. This is where NATO ends.

It was cold and rainy as we set out on the long ride over very bad roads through dark forests to Sobibor. The Nazis had hidden it well. I kept thinking about how we were comfortably ensconced in a spacious van with plush seats, not making this trip crammed into cattle cars, as the Jews whose photos we had just seen in Wlodawa had done. Slowing down to view the outline of the former rail line into the camp, we saw that we were the only visitors. Sobibor is the least-developed memorial of the six camps we visited, but that makes it seem more like it might have been when the camp was in use. Although there were revolts at all the camps, the one at Sobibor was the best planned and the most successful. There is a stone wall at the entrance with a plaque that states:

Kris-2 with photo on wall in Wlodawa

At this site between the years 1942 and 1943, there existed a Nazi Death Camp where 250,000 Jews and approximately 1000 Poles were murdered. On October 14th, 1943 during the armed revolt of the Jewish prisoners, the Nazis were overpowered and several hundred prisoners escaped to freedom. Following this revolt the Death Camp ceased to function.

"Earth conceal not my blood" Job

The well-planned revolt was led by Polish Jewish prisoner Leon Feldhendler and Soviet Jewish POW Alexander Pechersky, covertly killing eleven SS officers and several camp guards. About six hundred prisoners tried to escape through the barbed-wire fence, of whom about half made it through and onto the surrounding minefield. Soon many more were captured or killed. Ultimately a total of fifty prisoners survived the war. Himmler ordered the camp destroyed immediately following the uprising. The Nazis bulldozed the camp and planted pine trees in an attempt to hide all evidence of what had been perpetrated here. It is only in the past few months, since our return home, that the gas chambers have been located and their foundations unearthed, as well as a pendant inscribed in Hebrew dated 1927, earrings, and a wedding band engraved in Hebrew.

So there is little to see at Sobibor but so much for David and me to feel. The little museum building is shabby, with simple maps and posters explaining the history. There is a room devoted to the uprising and its survivors, and there we found photos of four Chelmers: Israel Chaim Trager, a bricklayer; Kalmen Wewerik, a carpenter; Schlomo Alster, a carpenter; and my hero, Ester Raab. Ester just died a few weeks ago in Israel. Before leaving the museum, we wrote a memorial message in the guestbook with the names of our Chelm families murdered here, we said kaddish, we held each other, and we cried. And then we began to walk through the camp in the downpour.

There is a long dirt path off to the left that is lined on both sides with small rocks. Each one has a black plaque attached, inscribed in white writing, and each one is a specific and heartbreaking memorial. In honor of them all, David and I made sure we read every one. Here are a few examples: "In memory of my mother Anna Godschalk born Zwaaf, my father Lion Godschalk, my grandfather Louis Godschalk, my grandmother Cornelia Godschalk born Jacobs, my grandfather Harog Zwaaf, my grandmother Clara Zwaaf born Zwaaf, May your souls be bound up in eternal life *** Louis Godschalk," "For the Unknown," "For the Zydow Chelmskich," "Mendel Morgenstern - Wlodawa July, 1942 Sobibor A young Rabbi who chose not to leave his children alone."

Sobibor memorial path with David

The rain intensified as we walked another long, muddy path to where there was a huge pyramid of sand mixed with ashes and crushed bones collected from the cremation pits. It was hard thinking that our families might have walked this same path to their death. David reached the low wall surrounding the area before me, and I saw his body fold over as he laid his head in his hands and sobbed. We said kaddish again. The tears from the skies mixed with the tears from our eyes. It was perfect.

Leaving Sobibor for the long van ride to return two Groman-Blajer family members to Chelm, we were subdued. The heavy rain continued, and the muddy roads deteriorated. Mapquest records that it is a thirty-six-mile distance, which should take forty-eight minutes. Mapquest has never made this trip. This is an extremely poor, rural part of Poland, and at times we were driving along what I believe were cow paths. Lots of tiny villages that had not changed since the nineteenth century lined the roadside, with their small wooden houses. It took several teeth-loosening hours before we reached a well-paved road and Kris announced that ahead was Chelm. David and I craned our necks, and there looming before us were the golden arches of McDonald's.

Chelm is the county capital of the Lublin district of Poland, with a current population of 67,546. It is sixteen and a half miles from the Ukrainian border. There is a rumor on Facebook that a Jewish couple moved there a few years ago. If true, that would make the Jewish population two. It is not a prosperous place, and most of the buildings are old, prewar, with a mix of some new commercial structures. The hotel was small and minimal, but we didn't care because we were finally here.

Months earlier online, I'd found a high school teacher in Chelm who is an expert on the Chelm Jews. His name is Zbigniew Lubaszewski, and I had asked Kris to arrange a meeting for us with him. The four of us met for dinner at the hotel. Zbigniew is extremely knowledgeable. As a historian, he is motivated by the belief that the reality of the prior existence of a Jewish community in Chelm must be known. He writes articles on the subject, gives talks on the radio, and has developed many databases. He is a highly dedicated man with a young family and says that many people are supportive of his work, though some are anti-Semitic and critical. He answered our questions and filled in a lot of information for us.

Most people who left Chelm in the 1920s and '30s went by train through Greece and Romania. We knew Bella and her children went through Italy but do not know Sam's route to Palestine. Zbigniew explained how complicated it would have been, even with the help of Zionist organizations, to get a certificate from the British Embassy in Warsaw. However, he told us, there were forged ones. The train station in Chelm had been blown up by the Nazis, but there are photos of it, and the rebuilt one is on the same site. There are also leaflets with photos of Jews who left, which can be bought at the town museum at 54 Lubelska Street, but the museum would not be open while we were in Chelm, which was disappointing.

We asked about the water works where Simon was a slave laborer, and he explained that in 1936 the works started to lay pipe to many parts of Chelm, and once the Nazis took it over, they used Jewish slave labor. I don't remember where I found it, but at some time in my research, I learned the name of the Nazi who was in charge of this project. His title was chief of the Chelm Water Works, and his name was Engineer Holzheimer.

At this dinner we learned from Zbigniew that the Chelm Ghetto had no fence or walls. It was a designated area where all Jews had to live. He also told us about the two-day liquidation of the ghetto, which was given as testimony by Poles who saw it. At this point we learned that Hersz Libhaber, killed on the second day, was buried in the mass grave in the Borek Forest with three hundred other Chelmers killed that day and sixty thousand Russian POWs who were starved to death in Stalag 319 on the outskirts of Chelm.

He told us that when the town's manager of streets learned that the action was to occur, he ordered that the streets adjoining the ghetto be barricaded so that no Jews could escape. This is when we found out that all cemetery records had been destroyed and that some broken headstones had been returned to the cemetery to make a memorial, but that has not yet been done.

A few hundred survivors returned to Chelm after the war, wanting to reinstate the community, but as happened in many places in Poland, some were killed by their former neighbors. The Jews formed small groups and stayed together, trying to get their houses back, but the authorities did nothing to help. One Jewish lawyer tried to represent them but only succeeded in getting his own house returned.

Zbigniew said that most Jews who lived here prewar were extremely poor. I was immediately reminded of my grandmother boiling pots of water to make it appear that she had food to cook. There was one small wooden house on Katowska Street where 120 people lived. I made Kris interpret this for me several times, to make sure I understood the number correctly. Recently there have been events in Chelm where Jewish music and food was presented and received positively. We ended this dinner with a promise from Zbigniew that he would do research for us that night on his databases and would guide us through Chelm for a few hours the next day. He graciously gave me his e-mail address and encouraged me to contact him in the future.

Friday, May 16, 2014—On the second floor of the Chelm Library building are the Chelm archives. We arrived early and spent six nonstop hours poring over ledgers containing addresses, inheritors of property, and reported changes of address, looking for family names. There is nothing modern about the system. The ledgers are huge volumes, handwritten in Polish, and it is impossible to review the pages easily unless you are standing over them. So for six hours I stood transfixed and never noticed the time. Kris helped with translation. Some of the records were two sided and some four sided. They demonstrated attempts by survivors to reclaim family property after the war. Here are some I found containing family names:

Arlene scanning ledger in Chelm

The property at 16 A Pieracki Street was owned by a Jankel and Perla (née Nissenbaum) Burstyn. Jankel died in 1921, and Perla died in November 1942 (the Action) in Chelm. The property was left to Joseph Rosenwijga, a nephew who was the son of Perla's sister Fajga, who married a Rosenweijga.

Confirmation by the tax office on November 3, 1945, that Hena Libhaber died June 2, 1943, in Majdanek, and her property was willed to her daughters, Ceperza and Gali Libhaber.

Recorded on July 20, 1946, that Wolf Tuchschnajder owned property about ten miles outside of Chelm and that he died in 1944 (note: after liberation of Chelm), leaving his property to Lejba Ruvina Blajer, the nephew of his daughter-in-law. Ita Myrla Groman married a Srul Wolf Tuchschnajder. Is this he? If so or not, the only relative left after the war to inherit was not a child, grandchild, sibling, or in-law. A Tuchschnajder had married a Blajer and a Lejba at that! There is the signature of Lejba Blajer on this record from 1946, so we've found another Blajer survivor.

Itzak Tuchschnajder died in Chelm in 1942, and his son, Wolf, inherits his property and is alive in 1946.

Recorded in 1947: Fishel Moszek Burstyn was married to Rywa (née Rubenstein) Burstyn and in 1936 lived at 12a Bednarska Street. Both died in the Chelm Ghetto, Rywa in 1941 and Fishel in August 1942. He left his property at 117 Lubelska Street to Abram Hersz Burstyn, son of his brother.

A property at 17 Kolejowa Street was owned jointly by Mayer Alios, Chana Gitla (née Alios) Libhaber, and Nuta Alios. Mayer owned 50 percent and Chana and Nuta 25 percent each. Mayer died on September 30, 1942; Chana died on August 27, 1942; and Nuta on November 1, 1939. The inheritors of Mayer's share were his children, Alice and Abram; of Chana's her son Icka Libhaber; of Nuta's his nephew Icka Libhaber.

A property ledger from 1936–1938 contained the following:

Srul Blajer managed property at 10 Lwoska and lived at 38 Pocztowa.

In 1936, Benecian Tuchznadjer [this is Ita Groman's father-in-law] sold 23 Lwowska Street to Josef Pasierbih and Sabina Iwaniek.

Chil Groman, my great-grandfather, owned, worked, and lived at 14 Katowska Street. The building was managed by Chawa Groman [Is that daughter Chana? If not, who is she?] and then by Lar Michal. Why the change of managers? What happened to Chawa or Chana Groman?

Bajla Libhaber owned and lived at 5 Ogredowa and then rented to Maria Bialan.

Jacob Szolma Tuchsznajder managed 37 Krzywa.

Nuta Burstyn lived at 25 Kopernika.

Kris explained that the next massive ledger was a record of where people moved to. Polish law at the time required that citizens who moved reported how many people were moving, their current address, and then, when they moved, their new address. Ultimately this ledger was the most astounding.

Jankel Burstyn, one person, from 4 Artyleryjska in Chelm to 4 Rembertow near Warsaw on January 27, 1933. Is this our Jankel who survived? In order to have wound up in Auschwitz and Gross-Rosen, our Jankel Burstyn would have had to leave Chelm before 1939.

Pessa Apelbaum, one person, moved from 64 Lubelski to 6 Twarda in Warsaw in December 1932.

Jochet Libhaber, one person; she had a business and lived at 5 Ogrodowa and in 1932 moved to 9 Zamenhof in Warsaw.

Szmul-Uszer Rajman, one person, moved from 34 Lubelska to the village of Karolinow in 1933.

Arom Tuchsznajder, one person, moved from 23 Lwowska to 29 Dr. Izoebski in Rozycze County [now Belarus] in 1933.

Lejba Tuchnajder, one person, moved from 5 Cicha to the Kowelski District in 1933.

Szajndla Tuchnajder, one person, moved to 29 Pawia in Warsaw in 1933.

Srul Lejba Blajer, one person, moved from 38 Pocztowa Street in Chelm to Biala Podlaska, 22 Narutocza in 1934.

Szmul Libhaber, one male and two females, moved from 27 Ogrodowa to Motodotyvil, Zmudz County in 1934.

Tauchim Lyb Rajman, one person, moved to 20 Ogrodowa in 1934.

Ita Tuchsznajder, one person, moved to 1 Chlodna in 1934.

Aron Joseph Libhaber, one person, had his business and residence at 5 Ogrodowa in 1934.

Lejba Burstyn, one person, lived at 32 Ogrodowa in 1934.

Abram Diament, one person, lived at 5 Katowska in 1934.

Tauba Burstyn, one person, moved from 32 Kopernika to Warsaw in 1937. Is this my great aunt Tauba on her way to Mexico City? Did she not inform the Chelm office for a year?

Sura and Chaim Apelbaum lived at 8 Pilarska in 1938.

Cipa Burstzyn, one person, lived at 29 Reformacka in 1938.

Lemel Tuchsznajder, one person, lived at 3 Pilichonki in 1938.

Chaia Pene Diament, one person, lived at 27 Lubelska in 1938.

Hersz Diament, one person, lived at 18 Lubelska in 1938.

Abram Apelbaum, one person, lived at 40 Kapernika in 1938.

Daniel Burstyn, one person, lived at 32 Kapernika and moved to Warsaw in 1938.

Mordechaj Rajman, one person, lived at 21 Lwowska and moved to Gesia Street in Warsaw in 1938.

My heart was beating faster as I searched for family names among the relocating Jews of Chelm in 1938, knowing what was coming for them in a year. Then the information on the pages began to change significantly. By then, some of them also knew what might be coming. Hitler had invaded, though he had mostly been welcomed, into Austria.

Mala Bursztyn, one person, moved from 36 Pocztowa to Argentina in 1938.

Chil Szmul Apelbaum, one person, moved from 21 Lubelska to Argentina in 1938.

Abram Chaim Nisenbaum moved to France in 1939.

The column of "place moved to" by Jewish Chelmers was changing. By 1938 they were leaving for the countryside and by 1939 for foreign countries—Palestine, Belgium, France, Argentina, Mexico.

And then it happened. I turned the page to 1940, and there it was, a visual representation of the Holocaust. At first I didn't know what I was seeing.

Basia Rajman, one person, lived at 6 Poctowa, moved to Zwarta in 1940.

Josef Bursztyn lived at 66 Kolejowa, moved to Zwarta in 1940. The whole long column, page after page, said Jews moved to Zwarta. I asked Kris what Zwarta meant. It means *died*.

We left the archives and met up with Zbigniew, who guided us on a fascinating walking tour of the old Jewish neighborhoods of Chelm, where there are many prewar and nineteenth-century buildings mixed in among newer ones. Earlier in the year, David and I had tried to find some of our family addresses on Google Earth. Although all the streets are still there, some of the addresses had disappeared, such as Chil Groman's. But Abram Hersz Blajer's business address is now a bank.

Walking the streets where our family lived and worked was exhilarating, as Zbigniew pointed out the buildings that had been the Jewish school, the recreation center, and the nineteenth-century wooden sleep porches hanging off the side of the once-opulent mansion. We walked past a police station and asked if there were any other police stations in Chelm. This was the only one and had always been here in this once-Jewish area. David and I were amazed to be walking just where our father had been attacked by the dog while walking to school as a little boy.

There was a building in ruins that had been a synagogue and another large building across the street that has a plaque on it saying that it had been a synagogue. It is massive and in good repair, and above the second story, the painted-over outline of the Hebrew Ten Commandments tablets can still be seen. A large sign over the front door says "Mackenzie's Saloon."

MacKenzee's Saloon

Lubelska Street is a main avenue filled with shops, and on one corner is a large multistory house, which Zbigniew told us is only house that is still owned by a Jewish family. They don't live in Chelm but rent it out and visit once a year. I assume it is the one that the lawyer who survived was able to reclaim.

There was one street corner that was particularly interesting. One side had several of the oldest and shabbiest nineteenth-century houses in a row. On the opposite corner was a gracious old mansion with a plaque denoting that this was Szmul Zygielbojm's home when he lived in Chelm as an elected leader of the Bund political party.

We had seen the memorial to Zygielbojm (1895–1943) at the Warsaw Ghetto. He had escaped Poland and become a member of the National Council of Poland on behalf of his party as part of the Polish government in exile in England. He devoted himself to informing the world about what the Germans were doing to the Polish Jews, as he was privy to information being smuggled out of Poland by Karski and others. He sent appeals to the Allies, letters to

Roosevelt, and made speeches on the BBC. He even wrote a book titled *Stop Them Now: German Mass Murder of the Jews of Poland.* All of his efforts were ineffective. After the collapse of the Warsaw Ghetto uprising, on May 13, 1943, Zygielbojm committed suicide to protest the inaction of the Allies. He left this:

> I can not stay alone. I can not live while the remnants of the Jewish people of Poland, which I represent, are eliminated. My comrades in the Warsaw ghetto fell with arms in their hands in the last heroic battle. I was not judged to die like them, with them. But I belong to them and their mass graves. By my death I wish to express the strongest protest against the passivity with which the world watches and permits the destruction of the Jewish people.

Directly across the street on the opposite corner is the brick side of a large building. There we saw graffiti, including a Jewish star. We asked Zbigniew what these large letters said. He told us they said "fuck the Jews."

"Fuck the Jews" graffiti in Chelm

From there we drove to the Jewish Cemetery, which was completely destroyed by the Nazis and had been so crowded before the war that there were plans to build a new one. After the war it was used as a park but now has a new wrought-iron fence with Jewish stars on the gate and a Holocaust memorial built by some Israeli Chelmers, including Sobibor survivor Ester Raab. There are some new memorial headstones and pieces of recovered ones. As we wandered through the tall grass, we occasionally found a partly-buried broken headstone. We knew we were walking over the ground where generations of our family are buried. We said kaddish. Leaving the cemetery, we drove past the location of the railway station where the journey to Sobibor began. Yesterday we had seen where it ended.

Saturday, May 17, 2014—After breakfast we left Chelm with a strong sense of fulfillment and a certainty that we would never return. Driving toward Belzec, I asked Kris to stop at Izbica, so I could see the train station and the tracks. The station building has not changed since the war. It was eerily empty as we drove by. During the Nazi roundups, conditions on the platform were so horrible that when Jan Karski saw the hordes of desperate people waiting for transport, he believed he had seen a concentration camp. They were Jews waiting for the trains to Belzec, which, like Sobibor and Treblinka, was a death camp where it is estimated that 450,000 Jews were murdered.

Because it was a death camp, there were only five or six survivors. Just two, Rudolf Reder and Chaim Hirszman, gave testimony. After Reder gave his testimony and wrote a book, he immigrated to Canada, suffered lifelong depression, and never talked about Belzec again. Hirszman remarried, as his first wife had been murdered at Belzec, and on March 19, 1946, he gave testimony before the regional historical council in Lublin. His testimony was adjourned, to be continued the next day. Hirszman was murdered that night, probably not because he was a Jew but because he was a communist. His wife resumed testifying on his behalf, reporting what he had told her.

There were, however, many other witnesses, as the camp was constructed very near the town of Belzec. There is an excellent documentary titled *Belzec* that is worth watching. Many Poles worked on the construction. The commandant lived in a house in the town; the Ukrainian camp guards, called the *Trawniki*, socialized and got drunk in town and, against orders, talked about what was happening. One man in the film recalls hanging around the railroad station, watching trains filled with Jews begging for water as the train cars waited their turn to enter the camp. People who lived nearby remember having to stay indoors, as the overwhelming stench of bodies stacked on pallets being burned was unbearable. I had seen the film before going to Poland, but it was made when archaeologists were first uncovering the site that had been destroyed by the Nazis and covered over with a forest. I knew that the site was now a finished memorial, and I was not disappointed as the Belzec Memorial was the most dignified, creative, and evocative of any of the six camps we visited.

The museum is excellently curated. As you enter the building, you walk down a long, narrow concrete hallway, reminiscent of the tube to the gas chamber, with large photos of victims suspended overhead. The rooms of the museum are impressively educational and filled with compelling exhibits. One that haunts me is a quote high up on a wall: "Mommy, haven't I been good? It's dark. It's dark." Here are a few of the texts accompanying the exhibits.

> In mid-March 1942 some 75 to 80 percent of all Holocaust victims were still alive, while 20 to 25 percent had perished. A mere eleven months later, in mid-February 1943, the percentages were exactly reversed.

FATE OF RELIGIOUS COMMUNITIES

The Germans publicly humiliated religious Jews who, because of their distinctive garb and appearance, were the most easily identified as Jews. Beards and earlocks were cut, and their clothing was reduced to shreds. Synagogues with their sacred Torah scrolls and religious books were burned. Jewish holidays were often chosen for German actions in order to further humiliate Jews and force them to desecrate Judaism. The results of these activities were clear: demoralization, despair, and above all, fear.

[Arrivals]

The receiving of the train began. Dozens of SS men would open the wagons, yelling "Los!" (Get out!). With whips and their rifle butts, they pushed people out. The doors of the wagon were a meter or more above the ground. Driven out by whips, the people had to jump down; everybody, old and young; many broke their arms and legs falling down. They had to jump down to the ground. The children were mangled in the bedlam. Everybody pouring out—dirty, exhausted, terrified …

With each transport it was the same as with the one that I arrived on. People were told to undress, leave their things in the courtyard … People always showed a spark of hope in their eyes that they were going to work. But seconds later, babies were torn away from their mothers, the old and the sick were thrown on stretchers, and the men, little boys, and girls were pushed with rifle butts further and further down the path. —Rudolf Reder

Inside [the gas chamber], the people were still standing erect, like pillars of basalt, since there had not been an inch of space for them to fall or even lean. Families could still be seen holding hands, even in death. It was a tough job to separate them as the chambers were emptied to make way for the next batch. The bodies were tossed out, blue, wet with sweat and urine, the legs soiled with feces and menstrual blood. A couple of dozen workers checked the mouths of the dead, which they tore open with iron hooks ... Other workers inspected anuses and genital organs in search of money, diamonds, gold, etc. Dentists moved around hammering out gold teeth, bridges, and crowns. In the midst of them stood Captain Wirth, in his element. Showing me a large can full of teeth, he said, "See for yourself. Just look at the amount of gold there is! you can't imagine what we find every day." —Kurt Gerstein

Kurt Gerstein (1905–1945)

Kurt Gerstein was both an SS man and an invaluable witness who released information about the Nazi killing center in 1942. As an SS *Untersturmführer* [second lieutenant] in the Technical Disinfections Department of the Hygienic Institute of the Waffen-SS, he worked directly with Zyklon B. Before the war, Gerstein was twice arrested for activities that diverged from Nazi views. Gerstein visited the Aktion Reinhard camps of Belzec and Treblinka in August 1942. Thereafter he passed information about what he saw to diplomats from

Sweden and the Vatican and to a bishop of the anti-Nazi German Confessing Church. In April 1945, Gerstein surrendered to French authorities. He provided two statements that included accounts of his visit to Belzec. For reasons that are not completely clear, he committed suicide in July 1945 while still in French custody.

Underground report based on information gathered by Dr. Janusz Peter, prisoners in the Belzec Sonderkommando [Jewish labor detachment] rebelled on June 13, 1942, and killed several SS guards. In response, the Germans killed all the prisoners who participated in the revolt. The revolt in Belzec has not been confirmed by other sources. Reports like this eventually found their way to the Polish government-in-exile in London, which in turn informed the Allies about the existence of Belzec. The Allies did not respond to these or other reports.

Of the more than 200 Trawniki-trained guards, who were aiding the murder process at Belzec, some tried to abandon their cruel service. In March 1943, fifteen guards deserted Belzec, and another detachment was sent from Trawniki to replace them. The new detachment mutinied in April, and its active participants were executed. New troops were recruited in east Galicia and assigned to guard the site.

The last exhibit is an experiential one, which is at the foot of the entry tunnel, as were the gas chambers. There is a huge metal door. Opening it, we entered a vast, very dark concrete room. There was one light placed on the floor, which created our shadows, and as we slowly walked toward the back of the room, our shadows got larger and larger, filling the chamber like ghosts. It was an emotionally powerful experience.

As we left the museum building, the sun was shining, but on the horizon the clouds were black, and large bolts of lightning created loud thunder. The storm was heading our way, but David and I were determined to enter the site of the camp. Kris provided us with an umbrella and chose to remain in the van.

When excavated it was revealed that the soil is very sandy, and as a result, all of the burial pits had migrated over time, creating one mass grave covering the entire area. To keep people from walking on it, walls were built around the site, and a path was created down the center.

Belzec path into mass grave

As we walked down the path, the sound of thunder got closer, and the walled sides got higher and higher. By the end of the pathway, we were deep inside the mound and confronting a memorial wall with Jewish first names. At the top of the wall is inscribed, "Let there be no resting place for my outcry! —Job." We lit our candle and said kaddish and then ascended the stairway to the top of the site, overlooking its vast expanse, completely covered and piled with black, charred rocks covering the entire mass grave. We held our breath. The rain increased, and the thunder grew louder as we made our long way back. Just as we approached the van, the storm changed course, and the sun returned.

Next stop was something wonderful—the beautiful Italian Renaissance-designed town of Zamosc. Rosa Luxemburg was born there. The main part of the magnificent synagogue has been restored to its former glory but again is a museum filled with relics and, this time, computer kiosks explaining the history of Zamosc. The large town square, filled with cafés and surrounded by exquisite colorfully decorated buildings, was a photographer's feast and certainly brightened our mood.

The good mood continued as we drove through the glorious, sunny countryside surrounded by fields of canola plants in full, yellow bloom. Kris had a treat for us as he pulled off the road and parked behind a quaint little house constructed of logs and straw. It was a charming restaurant, owned by a lovely woman who is a friend of Kris. Nestled at a cute table, the three of us ate a delicious lunch consisting of mushroom soup, three types of pierogi, schnitzel with a fried egg atop, boiled new potatoes, and apple fritters for dessert. Total cost was forty dollars for all three. We insisted on thanking the cook, who emerged from the kitchen and blushed as we complimented her culinary skill.

Back in the van, we drove through villages and towns and repeatedly learned that this place had been 60 percent Jewish and that place had been 100 percent Jewish and the other place had been 40 percent Jewish, and now there were none. That information was shared constantly throughout the trip and deepened our sense of the enormity of what the Nazis had perpetrated.

By midafternoon we arrived in the city of Lublin and a much better class of hotel. Lublin was a delightful surprise, with its cosmopolitan atmosphere coupled with Old World charm. We walked the large cobblestone streets lined with shops and cafés and admired the many beautiful old buildings. Many of them had been restored, while some had not, as their Jewish ownership was still in dispute.

Huge squares and city gates led to a castle that had been used by both the SS and the KGB for interrogations but was now an art museum. That night it was crowded with people enjoying free admission, and everyone was in high spirits. Sitting on the balcony of a café overlooking the large park below, we snacked on onion rings and chicken wings. Kris explained that the park was once the Jewish neighborhood, which had been totally destroyed. We wandered back to our hotel, looking forward to a good shower and a comfortable bed.

Sunday, May 18, 2014—Majdanek concentration camp is located on the outskirts of Lublin, and there were few visitors when we arrived early Sunday morning. It was a large compound, so it was startling to learn that what we were seeing was only one fifth of what had originally existed. There is a humongous stone memorial at the entrance. The Nazis opened the camp in September 1941, and it was liberated by the Soviets in July 1945. During that period 360,000 people died or were killed here; of these, 120,000 were Jews.

David and I took a long walk through the camp, entering various buildings and wooden barracks. Majdanek looks like what you expect a concentration camp to look like, except there is grass now instead of mud. Here we saw the kinds of slave labor those who were not immediately killed were forced to do. We went into the gas chamber and the barracks, where thousands of shoes were displayed, crammed into floor-to-ceiling wire cages. In one barracks there were toys and dolls that had been confiscated and a display of all the different badges that prisoners had to wear: the pink triangle for homosexuals, the black circle for criminals, the yellow star for Jews, the purple triangle for Jehovah's Witnesses, the black triangle for Roma, and many others. There were photographs of people who had been murdered, and we stopped to say kaddish. Another barracks is dark and filled with lights encased in barbed-wire balls. It serves as a shrine. Barracks crowded with wooden-tiered bunks seemed almost familiar.

As we made our way, we were approached by two young women who stopped us. In a friendly manner, they explained that they were Seventh-Day Adventists and were here because the Nazis had murdered so many of their faith. Then they offered us pamphlets, which we declined. We continued to the back of the camp, where the crematorium stands with its tall chimney and row of ovens. Next to it is a very big monument atop a wide, high staircase. A mausoleum atop the stairs is formed as a giant concrete bowl with a huge dome covering the contents from the elements. The contents are an immense pile of human ashes. We threw our stones on the pile and said kaddish once more. The inscription on the dome says: OUR FATE IS A WARNING TO YOU.

Our next stop was at the famous old *yeshiva* in Lublin, which is a magnificent yellow-and-white building. It has been restored and now is mostly occupied by the Ilan Hotel, whose slogan is "Feel the Tradition." There is a Polish guard who knew Kris and escorted us with great enthusiasm on a wonderful tour of the part of the building that is once again a yeshiva. It was founded by the famous Rabbi Shapiro in 1931, with a huge dedication celebration.

It was a seven-year school that admitted boys at age fourteen. In order to be accepted to the yeshiva, one had to know two hundred folios of Babylonian Talmud by heart. The most gifted and the poorest students received scholarships. At Rabbi Shapiro's funeral on October 29, 1933, thirty thousand Jews from all over Poland took part.

The yeshiva has been beautifully restored, though it now occupies just a fraction of its former space and has an active synagogue community consisting of fourteen men and seventeen women who are waiting for a rabbi from Israel to come to certify the restored *mikvah.* Today there are three students.

Kris drove us to a very chic, upscale restaurant in Lublin for lunch. Its ultramodern decor, highly polished surfaces, mirrors, and black and red fabrics seemed more like downtown New York City. I indulged in a favorite which, since the outbreak of mad cow disease, is no longer on menus at home: an elaborately prepared tableside dish of steak tartare. It was quite a contrast with dinner that night, which was at Andragora, a kitschy Jewish restaurant in the heart of Lublin. The place is filled with Jewish memorabilia, photographs, klezmer music, and treadle sewing machines; the waitresses dressed in nineteenth-century peasant garb. The food, of course, was familiar fare.

Monday, May 19, 2014—In the morning, Kris led us to the foot of the Brama Grodzka Gate, which had separated the Christian and Jewish sections of Lublin. There we entered the NN Theatre, which now houses the archives of Lublin's Jewish life and serves as an educational center to teach children about the Holocaust. It was the first time our nervous young guide had given an extensive tour of the facilities. Our group consisted of David, me, and a German woman and her teenage son, neither of whom ever spoke a word. NN stands for No Name and is so called after a Jewish girl who lived under the Brama Gate when her parents were deported. The little child did not remember her name but believed she had a brother. She was given to a gentile family.

Of the forty thousand Jews in Lublin, three hundred survived the war. The guide talked about how the water supply was turned off to the ghetto, and there was only one distant well where people lined up for hours to get water to carry the long distance back to their homes. Kris had shown us the old pumping well yesterday, which is now surrounded by a parking lot.

The most amazing and powerful exhibit is the prewar photographs and the story of how they got to be here. In May 2012 the Grodzka Gate—NN Theatre Center received a collection of more than 2,700 glass-plate negatives in various sizes. The photographs were taken between 1914 and 1939 by a professional photographer. They were found by workmen doing repairs in the attic of a house at 4 Rynek Street.

So after many decades, from a dark hiding place emerged the faces of the people of Lublin before the outbreak of war. The pictures show individuals and groups indoors or in garden settings—at work and at play. Adults and children and family photos documenting major events of family life, along with pictures of the Jewish school, Jewish cemetery and gravestones, teachers, students, tailors, firemen, road builders, bridges, churches, carts, and a steam engine. Very few label the people in them. The photographer had not been identified when we were there but has been recently. His name is Abram Zylberberg, and he was fifty-six years old when the Germans invaded. Unable to save himself, he saved his life's work. Seventy-three years later, it reveals in superb images the life of a now nonexistent town.

The guide spoke about Poles who were righteous and saved Jews, risking their own lives. He never mentioned anything about anti-Semitic Poles or those who were perpetrators. When I later told Kris about this, he said that the staff of the NN is under attack by anti-Semites.

Leaving Lublin, we were on our way to Sandomierz, hoping we could get there. There had been serious flooding of the Vistula River, and the way might be blocked. Luckily we made it through, although there were soldiers at checkpoints, and we drove over some bridges where the water almost reached the roadbed.

The Sandomierz Cathedral houses the infamous eighteenth-century "Blood Libel" painting. The blood libel is the irrational and groundless belief promulgated by the Russian Orthodox and Catholic Church since medieval times that Jews ritually murder Christian children and use their blood to make matzah for Passover. This absurd belief has been responsible for the raping and killing of countless Jews and for justifying pogroms. Though the church has long ago denounced this as a falsehood, the myth persists in many places. So I wanted to see this grotesque work for myself, although I had seen reproductions. The guidebook states that there now is a disclaimer posted next to the painting.

The town of Sandomierz is breathtakingly terraced on a steep hillside. The cathedral was very impressive but closed on Mondays, so we could not see the painting. But all was not lost. Kris proceeded to take us down the street to what had been the synagogue, which now houses ages of the district's archives. That turned out to be a truly remarkable experience. While we waited near the entrance, Kris convinced the clerk to let us in and show us around.

The clerk produced a huge iron key, and we were led to a mammoth iron door, which he unlocked. We entered a large tall room that had been the synagogue sanctuary. It was filled from floor to ceiling with metal scaffolding that could be climbed to the upper levels. The levels were packed with shelves holding thousands of ledgers and boxes of documents, some of which were spilling onto the floors. There was barely any room to walk around this structure, and so we climbed up. We were in awe of what we found painted on the surrounding walls, almost close enough to touch. Fading but still visible were colorful frescos that had decorated the synagogue sanctuary. Near the ceiling, which must have been above the ark, were the tablets of the Ten Commandments. Kris randomly opened some of the ledgers of residents, and there were the records of countless Jewish families among the Christians. We perused a page of Kestenbergs: Chaja Ruchla, Hinda Laja, Gitla Hena, Chaskiel Majer, Jakob, and on and on. David and I were overcome to be in such a place, where very few people ever go.

Sandomierz archives

The Sandomierz town square looks like a picture from a fairy tale, with its charming little shops and cafés and central bell tower. But it has a brutal past. As the town is on a hill, the square slopes down. The square is where seven thousand to nine thousand Jews were rounded up and then beaten so viciously that their blood

115

ran down the slope and filled this huge place before they were transported to Treblinka.

We drove to Krasnik to visit two synagogues that are being converted to museums and then on for hours through lush, hilly countryside, with the majestic Carpathian Mountains in the distance. Endless shtetls appeared, with their mix of the old and new dwellings, many old people using bicycles for transportation and women wearing babushkas. Each place had a Catholic cemetery, ablaze with displays of multicolored artificial flowers on every grave, as if an artificial flower factory had exploded overhead. It seemed to me to reflect a competition among the inhabitants as to who loved their departed most. Kris validated that perception.

The drive continued onto some very poorly maintained, narrow roads shared with lots of huge truck traffic. This made for some nervous moments, and then suddenly we were on a superhighway. Entering Galicia, I spotted the first mileage sign for the city of Oswecium (the Germans named it Auschwitz) and felt a bit anxious. Kris had warned us that since Auschwitz is the number-one tourist attraction in Poland, it gets very crowded. Most tourists approach on buses from Krakow, arriving late in the morning. To beat the crowds and get to the camp early the next day, he proposed that we spend the night in Oswecium. We agreed, and as we entered the city, we saw a billboard announcing an upcoming Eric Clapton concert. The hotel was poor, with a thin, lumpy mattress, but so luxurious compared to the bunks our fellow Jews had endured nearby that we dared not complain. And yes, among a few black-humored jokes to disguise our anxiety, we took showers.

Tuesday, May 20, 2014—Because we arrived at Auschwitz early, it was not the mob scene it would later become. Auschwitz was the largest German concentration camp and death camp. Between 1940 and 1945, at least 1,300,000 people were deported to Auschwitz, of whom 1,100,000 were Jews. Of the 1,100,000 people who died in Auschwitz, 90 percent of the victims were Jews. Auschwitz, which has blocks of brick buildings, was originally a prison before the

Nazis arrived. In 2012 it had 1.43 million visitors and therefore is organized in a way that is reminiscent of a theme park. We lined up to get our tickets, and then were called into a group with an English-speaking guide. Our group was small, as it was early, so there were only about twenty of us. David and I were the only Jews in the group. The guide was a young Polish man, who was excellent at his job and had an obvious passion for his work. We walked into the camp under the famous ironic wrought-iron words *ARBEIT MACHT FREI* (work makes you free). These words are not exclusive to the Auschwitz camp. There was a drawing displaying the band of musicians who played at the entrance in the morning and evening as the slave laborers marched out and back each day. The cobblestone pathways were uneven and a bit difficult to travel.

Entering various blocks, the history and artifacts of Auschwitz were detailed and displayed—room after room full of masses of hair, shoes, spoons, eyeglasses, wheelchairs, crutches, knives, forks, bowls, toys, dolls, shaving brushes, leg braces, shoe polish, canes, hairbrushes, toothbrushes, combs stacked up by the thousands. And then the piles of old tattered leather and cardboard luggage and briefcases; as part as the deception, identifying information had been written on the outside of each piece, to give the false assurance that belongings would be returned after disinfection showers. Now we were not just looking at anonymous items but suitcases belonging to L. Berman from Hamburg 26.12.1886, Margarete Glaser 14.8.1897, Klara Sara Goldstein, Judith Gelder Cohen from Holland 13.12.1883, Else Meier from Koln Sep. 1892, Berta Sara Lenzberg from Wein, Hanna Minska, Herman Pasternak from Germany 1900, L. Weinberg 4.8.1936.

We saw the cells, the interrogation rooms, and one block where no photographs were allowed because it was as it had been originally. There in the basement were small starving cells where prisoners were put to starve to death and another tiny cell that was called a standing torture cell. Prisoners had to crawl into it through a small opening near the floor and share the space with enough others that it was packed. Everyone had to stand all night long before crawling out to go to work the next day. Daily ration of food contained 1,500 calories, while prisoners had to work approximately eleven hours every day.

We went to the execution wall, where there were some memorial flowers. David and I began to be disturbed by what was to become a familiar scene. A young Japanese couple in our group was posing with cheerful smiles in front of the wall.

Many of the blocks were very well curated, with lots of important photographs and information. Here's an example:

Prisoners held in the concentration camp died from overwork, starvation, sadistic punishments, exhaustion after prolonged roll-calls, torture, appalling living conditions, being used for medical experiments, or arbitrary execution. Those too weak or sick to work were picked out by the SS during roll-calls or in the infirmary and sent to the gas chambers or murdered with phenol injections.

The work was mostly hard labor, such as working in a stone quarry, but a preferred job was working in what the prisoners called "Canada." Their job was to sort through the piles of prisoners' civilian clothes, looking for jewelry and other hidden valuables that could make you rich, just like living in Canada, if you could keep it. Of course, if caught, keeping anything you found could get you killed, but some prisoners managed to obtain some money that they used to ease their lives in the camp.

There were uprisings and attempted escapes from Auschwitz, as there were at most camps. Girls working as slave laborers at a munitions factory had smuggled explosives into the camp on their bodies, and with these supplies, other prisoners were able to blow holes in the crematorium. Three of the girls were tortured and later hanged beside the road, where all prisoners would see them as they passed by.

Walking toward the gas chamber, we were near the fence behind which Rudolf Hoss and his wife and five young children lived. Hoss was the camp commander, and his children played in the yard behind the fence. There was also a gallows nearby, where Hoss had been hanged on April 16, 1947. By now the camp was getting more crowded, and we waited in line a bit to enter the gas chamber, which held one large vase of flowers in the center of the floor. From there we went into the crematorium, with its wall of ovens.

Auschwitz gas chamber

Slowly we made the long walk back to the entrance, where our group boarded the shuttle bus to Birkenau. It is a distance of about two miles between the two camps. At Birkenau the railroad tracks run right into the camp, and the prisoners arrived at a special unloading ramp. Women and children were immediately separated from men. The selection of those who were deemed fit for work was carried out by SS doctors and directed to the camp. This amounted to about 25 percent of the arrivals. The remainder were taken to the gas chambers. Personally I found Birkenau to be a more emotional experience than Auschwitz. Its wooden barracks, most with only their chimneys remaining, stretched on and on as far as one could see.

It was a very hot, sunny day, and it was a long walk to the unloading ramp, where a lone boxcar stood. Once again some people posed in front of train car for souvenir snapshots. From the ramp, we proceeded through the barbed-wire fence into the camp and walked back toward the remains of the gas chambers and crematorium, where we said kaddish. There is a pool of ashes surrounded by gravel, where a black granite slab reads: "To the memory of the men, women, and children who fell victim to the Nazi genocide. Here lie their ashes. May their souls rest in peace."

The long, low rows of wooden barracks that remain are chilling to enter. Interiors of some have brick walls dividing three tiers of bunks with wooden floors. The large barracks each held one small stove for heating. We were there on a hot day, and it was stifling inside. Seeing the stove reminded us of how unrelentingly cold the prisoners were in the winter. There are names scratched into the wood and the bricks, but it is not clear whether these are from inmates or tourists. One barracks holds the toilet facilities, which consisted of long rows of concrete with about fifty holes staggered back to back. Prisoners were allowed a limited time to use the holes and were sometimes shot for taking too long. The holes just filled with waste, and the best job in the camp was cleaning out the holes, because those workers were always covered with feces and smelled so bad that the guards would not go near them.

Birkeneau toilets

We had been at Auschwitz and Birkenau for almost four hours and were tired as we walked out of the camp, surrounded by the endless barbed-wire fences and wooden guard towers.

Kris drove us back town so we could visit the Auschwitz Jewish Center, which consists of the restored Chevra Lomdei Mishnayot

121

Synagogue and a newly constructed modern museum addition "to keep alive the memory of the Jewish residents of Oswiecim and to teach about the dangers of prejudice and discrimination." The museum addition had just opened two days before, and we were delighted to meet the woman who had designed it. According to the brochure:

> The synagogue was fully restored to its pre-war condition based on the testimonies and recollections of survivors and reopened to the public in 2000 ... Today it has it has neither a rabbi nor a local congregation; but as the only Jewish house of worship near Auschwitz, it is available to visitors for prayer, reflection, bar/bat mitzvahs, and other celebrations.

The displays in the synagogue exhibit artifacts and photographs of prewar life in Oswiecim (Oshpitzin in Yiddish). There is Judaica, found in 2004, buried beneath the site of the former Great Synagogue, which was destroyed by the Nazis. There are cases showing articles related to Jacob Haberfeld's business as a Spiritus-Raffinerie, Likor-Fabrik. A variety of colorful bottles of his alcohol products, letters written on his fancy letterhead, along with advertising ashtrays and coasters are on view. There are letterheads from businesses owned by Josef Bernstein and Isak Kanner and photographs of business associations, elementary school classes, and members of the socialist-Zionist political party. There are also photographs of individuals and families to connect us with prewar Jewish life here. From the first half of the sixteenth century until before the war, Oswiecim was almost 100 percent a Jewish town.

The modern addition focuses on exhibits relating to the war and its aftermath. It is a stark white, triangular space with a line of photographs of the faces of former residents running along the middle of the walls. These are some of the items contained in the cases beneath:

Street sign for Tischlerstrasse (Carpentry Street), 1939–1945. When World War II broke out, Oswiecim was incorporated into the Third Reich. The town was renamed Auschwitz and Polish street names were replaced with German ones. This street sign was located at Stolarska Street, which was renamed Tischlerstrasse, meaning Carpentry Street in German. The street sign was found during the archeological excavation of the site of the Great Synagogue in 2004. It provides a clear look at how the invading Germans erased the pre-war identity of Oswiecim, and of its citizens.

Identification papers stamped for JEW.

A pass for five Jewish men from Oswiecim to travel in order to bury a fallen Jewish soldier, issued by the town mayor, Dr. Emil Golczewski, September 7, 1939.

A letterhead from Pinkus Wassertheil Paper and Cardboard merchants while under operation by a German commissioner. Jewish stores, companies and factories were confiscated by the Germans in spring 1940.

Postcard sent by David Henneberg from Oswiecim to his relative, Zita Hennenberg Plaut and her husband Lutz Plaut, in New York, 1941. David Hennenberg informs Zita about the location of her parents and how to send packages. He also asks her to send him matzoh for Passover.

Eviction notice for Akiba Koschitzky, demanding he vacate his apartment … and appear by 8 a.m. on February 17, 1941, for resettlement outside the city. It says that he should bring his personal documents, enough food for three days, and luggage up to 25 kg.

German order of the demolition for the remnants of the Great Synagogue in Oswiecim, burned on November 29/30, 1939, given under strict penalty.

Henryk Enoch's notebooks from the 1940–1941 school year. Henryk Enoch was born in 1932 in Oswiecim and lived with his family at 8 Legionow Street. During World War II, he attended secret classes for

Jewish students, taught by Jadwiga Marciniak, a non-Jewish teacher at Queen Jadwiga Public School in Oswiecim. In 1941, Henryk was deported with his parents to the ghetto in Bedzin, where he died.

An article about the deportation of Jews from Oswiecim to Bedzin and Sosnowiec in the German-controlled Polish-language Jewish newspaper, *Gazeta Zydowska*, 1941. The propaganda article stresses the speed and good organization of the process, which deported over 5,000 people in 7 days.

A pass for Regina Grunbaum to return to Oswiecim, her hometown, after liberation from Bergen-Belsen, 1945.

There is a small, lovely cafe and museum shop and we were warmly welcomed by the young Polish couple who operate it. There are free booklets distributed explaining what a hate crime is and telling people how to report such a crime to the police and a website, www.reportracism.pl. The cover of the booklet states "We are determined to put an end to racial hatred in Poland. All we need is to let us know."

The drive from Oswiecim to Krakow was spectacular—several hours of winding through the Carpathian Mountains, huge lush valleys, and steep-roofed wooden houses so reminiscent of Switzerland. This is logging country, and piles of timber and truckloads of lumber were ever present. Kris had another treat to refresh us and drove up a small path into a beautiful garden and a stunning former abbey for a special three-course meal, which included my first taste of hare pate. The staff was delightful and most accommodating as Kris logged on to his laptop and downloaded lots of genealogical records for me onto a memory stick. We reviewed the data he had obtained.

This is when I learned of my Blayer great-grandmother Sura's 1931 death record and another surprise, the record of a request made in 1954 by Simon Libhaber to have his name and his parents' names on his birth record from 1922 changed. He requested Gitla become Gizela, Hersz become Henryk, and himself, Szolma Joel, become Szimon Jan. Later, when I asked his daughter Henrietta what she knew of this, she had no knowledge and did not even know that her father's middle name had originally been Joel. She speculated that under the communists in Poland in 1954, anti-Semitism was a big problem, and changing their names from the Jewish version to the Polish version may have been important in order to obtain employment.

We arrived in Krakow late in the afternoon and were very impressed by how beautiful the city is. It is a great old European city, which served as the capital of the Nazis' general government. Krakow was never bombed, and although the retreating Germans wired the city to be blown up, a Soviet spy learned of the plan and cut the wires.

No cars are allowed in the city center, and so we strolled through streets filled with fabulous architectural gems from a variety of periods, many restaurants, and internationally famous upscale shops flaunting their high-style wares. Magnificent medieval walls with their stupendous gates surround the inner city. We arrived at the town square and were amazed. Krakow's is the largest European town square, and it was filled with people, music, horse-drawn carriages, myriad cafés and nightclubs. It is a party city, and just as people at home may go to Las Vegas for bachelor parties and other celebrations, Europeans go to Krakow.

Kris, David, and I sat in a café drinking wine while taking in the circus around us, and I marveled at how the beginning and ending of just one day could encompass such extremely different experiences.

Wednesday, May 21, 2014—We woke knowing this was our last day in Poland but chose not to acknowledge it. Kris drove us to the Jewish section of Krakow, a large vibrant area that is the biggest tourist attraction in Poland after Auschwitz. For three hours we walked its cobblestone streets, past the Galicia Jewish Museum and the alley where part of *Schindler's List* was filmed. There was a bustling town square, with its Jewish Restaurant Café advertising kosher meals in English and Hebrew: Berdytchov soup, carp fish

Jewish style, roast goose, crispy roast duck with apples, *tcholent*, Passover cheese and kosher wine.

There was a plaque commemorating Chez Helena, the childhood home of Helena Rubenstein, and storefronts recreated to look like they had been before the war, with their folding wooden doors and signs: Babelsteins, Aron Weinberg's, Stanislaw Nowak's, and the Hamas and Happiness Book Store appeared a la Disney.

Kris escorted us into a building where there is a bookshop owned by a lovely couple that houses a huge inventory of Jewish books and Judaica. We spent a pleasant time with them, and it was here I purchased my only souvenir of the trip. It is a beautifully carved ten-inch-tall figure of a Hasidic klezmer musician. Leaving the shop, I spotted a posting attached to the hall wall. Here is what it said:

DO YOU RECOGNIZE ANY OF THESE PERSONS?
DO YOU HAVE ANY INFORMATION ABOUT THEM?
Other surnames connected with the SCHWARZER family:
TENNENBAUM, FEDER, LIEBERMAN.
The cities connected with this family: KRAKOW, CIESZANOW, GRODZISKO DOLNE.
Contact: adelaschwarzer@hotmail.com
www.adelaschwarzer.com or (Sweden)
+46 70 520 76 26 Jan, the son of Adela Schwarzer

Below this information there were nine photographs. One was of Adela and her two parents and then six other younger Schwarzers: Izak, born 1919; Gusta, born 1921; Helena, born 1925; Regina, born 1926; Samuel, born 1928; and Amelia, born 1930. All the faces smiling and reminding me of the endless postings that plastered the walls and buildings in Manhattan after 9/11. Desperate people were looking for lost loved ones, but this was sixty-nine years later, and Adela, with the help of her son and the Internet, is still searching.

There are seven synagogues in Krakow, and we saw them all. There is an impressive gate leading to the outer courtyard of the Remoh Synagogue, and the surrounding walls are filled with plaques.

> In memory of the Jewish martyrs of Cracow who were annihilated by the Nazi Germans in the terrible period 1939–1945. <u>EARTH DO NOT COVER THEIR BLOOD</u>
> In Memory of the Righteous Among Nations
> In memory of KAMSLER from the Kamsler Families
> AUSTRALIA
> In sacred and everlasting remembrance of the Ebner Family of Nowy Wisnicz who perished as victims of Nazi Atrocities
> This plaque is dedicated by
> MURRAY EBNER
> The only surviving family member of the Bochnia Ghetto
> Herschel ben Yitzchak Feigel bas Yehonoson
> Father Mother
> Brothers
> Avraham ben Herschel- Zizha ben Herschel-Nuta ben Herschel
> Yahrtzeits Observed 3 Elui
> Dedicated November 1, 2004 by Murray and Sylvia Ebner
> Lisa, Gayle, Aaron and Jared Rosen- Mark, Nicole, Zachary, Julian and Sabrina Ebner- Cynthia Ebner
> Columbus Ohio U.S.A.

Entering the richly decorated, small, crowded Remoh Synagogue, tourists climb the steps to the ark to kiss the red velvet curtain covering the Torah. Behind the synagogue stands the Jewish cemetery, and *stands* is definitely the correct term for it. The Nazis ordered the Jews to destroy the tombstones. The Jewish slave laborers merely tipped them all over. Today they all stand upright and wear metal hats. During the Communist era, acid rain in Krakow was the worst in all of Europe. To keep the headstones from being eroded, they were fitted atop with metal protectors.

Krakow headstone with 'hat'

There is a Ba Shem (holy man) and his family buried here in a fenced area, and there was a religious Jewish man praying at the site, which was covered with notes left by others who had prayed there. It was like the notes that are left crammed into the Western Wall in Jerusalem. Kris engaged the caretaker of the cemetery in conversation, and he explained that before the war there were sixty thousand Jews in Krakow. Only 250 of those Jews remain, and they are, of course, old. He also oversees an old-age facility for them, which is dependent on donations. I gave him a hundred dollars, and with enormous gratitude, he told Kris in Polish to tell me that he would pray "for the benefactor" every day.

We then walked to the building where the old-age home is located and the synagogue where Rabbi Eliezer Gurary from Israel has just become the new rabbi of Krakow. There is a mikvah, and the sign said that it is open Sunday through Friday 7:00 a.m.–8:00 a.m., Friday 5:30 p.m.–6:30 p.m., and Saturday 8:00 a.m.–9:00 a.m.

A resurgence of Jewish life in Krakow is occurring, and the community is growing. The Jewish Community Center boasts a large banner proclaiming "Building a Jewish Future in Krakow." There is a Jewish festival. We wandered to the open market along streets that have Jewish names—Estery, Meiselsa, Jozefa, and made our way to the Issac Synagogue, which is the home of Chabad Lubavitch in Krakow and advertised live klezmer music at 6:00 p.m. today, and then past a synagogue with enormous closed iron doors, which is no longer in use but did display a sign announcing an exhibit of Jewish Families of the Inter-War Cracow. Sadly, it was time to leave for our seven-hour ride back to Warsaw.

Kris, of course, had several stops lined up along the way back. Passing through shtetls, many of which had not changed much since before the war, we stopped to see a very large three-story brick ruin of a former synagogue. The roof was gone, and trees grew up through the interior and out what were once windows. To have once had such a impressive synagogue, there must have been a large Jewish population here, but what now remains is a decaying reminder of a lost civilization.

Decaying brick synagogue

As we drove through another town square, Kris pointed to a balcony on the second floor of a house and told us that he knew the woman who used to live there; she had hidden a young Jewish boy during the war. Somehow, focusing on the view of that balcony evoked a more physically painful emotional reaction in me than almost anything else I had seen during the trip. It was a very small town square, and the house stood right in the middle of it, so it seemed obvious that others must have known what this woman was doing, and yet no one gave her away. Maybe it was the heroism of this ordinary woman or a culmination of the emotions of a journey soon to be ended, but to this minute, the view of that little balcony brings tears to my eyes.

Nearby we drove past a huge Jewish cemetery that had not been destroyed but was also, though fenced and gated, overgrown. Then we had a fine lunch in a bucolic setting on a warm, sunny day, followed by a visit to a very impressive sculpture garden with some truly fine works, which was a refreshing change. Kris had taken us from destruction to the beauty of artistic creation before returning us to the Airport Marriott in Warsaw where, with enormous gratitude, we sadly said good-bye to him.

It was evening when we arrived, and David and I went for dinner in the hotel restaurant. The sense that our long-awaited trip was over was made stronger by our surroundings, which were the familiar, homogenized ambience of a chain hotel. Before the trip, I had thought about whether or not to talk with David about us, about our estrangement for many years. I decided I would see how our time together went and how we got along.

David was the perfect person to have shared this trip with. We are the only two people in the world who know what it felt like to grow up in our parents' home, and we both have had a lifelong passionate interest in European history and the Holocaust. David, in fact, has a master's degree in history and often was my search engine. Although we had not shared a bedroom since 1955, doing so every night had worked out smoothly. He went to sleep earlier than I, so I used that time to write the notes of the day on my iPad. He woke earlier in the morning and was out of the room by the time I needed to get dressed.

He was generous and thoughtful. There had been no difficult moments between us, and so with just a few hours left before we would be on our way home, I knew this was the best opportunity I might ever have to talk with him about what had happened. Why had we stopped communicating with each other for decades? I was willing to expose my reasons if he was willing to own his. He was. We talked intimately for a long time in an easy, loving manner and learned a great deal about each other. Misperceptions were addressed and apologies made, and there was a soft easiness between us.

There are many ways we all lose people, and this entire project from the very beginning had been about finding lost and unknown family and learning more about who they were and what had happened to them. In the process, we've found people in Australia, Mexico, Brazil, and Canada. We've traced our family back to the 1700s in Poland. We've found scores of relatives and learned many things about their lives, their community, and their deaths.

We found Jeff Groman, Bella's brother Izzy's grandson, living in Chicago, and I had a delightful hour-long phone conversation with him. He learned more about his Hebrew name, Joseph Yechiel, which he knew was in honor of his father Roberto's uncle Joe and brother Gil, but he did not know that Gil was named Yechiel in honor of our great-grandfather, Chil Groman. David and Jeff discovered that they live just a short distance apart. They had a family reunion brunch, and I sent David copies of Jeff's grandfather's birth and marriage records to give to him.

My correspondence with Sharon Groman and Henrietta Herzfeld continues to this day, and Henrietta and her husband, Morry, are coming from Melbourne to the United States and will meet Aunt Ruth while visiting New York City. They will spend a week with me and my family here in Buffalo in the fall. David and his partner, Bobbe, will join us. Henrietta wrote today that she has found someone to translate her grandmother Gitla's notebooks into English and will bring them with her. I am excited that we may find more information about what happened to the Groman family during the war and answers to many questions. I know this search has no end. But for me, the most important person I found doing this project is a man who lives a mere 473 miles away from me, my brother, David.

Afterword

Within days of returning to Buffalo, I was in Miami for the funeral of my beloved cousin Ellen Blaier Chopp. Another way we lose those we love. It pains me that she never got to know about the trip and that she will never read this.

I did keep my promise and returned to a meeting of the Yiddish group at the Jewish Senior Apartments. We met in a larger space this time, as word of my first presentation had spread and more folks wanted to attend. They were a great audience, eager to hear all about the trip and see the photographs I'd taken. I thoroughly enjoyed myself, and so did they.

After the presentation, many people came up to talk to me personally, and I noticed that Leonide, whom I had sat next to the first time I came to the group, was waiting by himself near the door. As I went to leave, he approached me, asking if I would like to come upstairs to his apartment and see some photographs. Having not been asked to a man's apartment in ages, I agreed—to the titters and delight of the others in the room. Leonide, from Belarus, was a soldier in the Red Army during the war, as were his four brothers. He wanted me to see a large framed photograph of the five of them in uniform that hangs prominently over his dining table.

He was a tank commander fighting the Japanese and pulled the leg of his pants up to show me where part of his leg is missing after being wounded. He told me that the doctors wanted to amputate, but he refused to let them. Leonide was passionate that people know many Jews were soldiers in the Red Army during the war. In fact, 1.5 million Jews fought with the Allies during World War II, 500,000 in the Red Army. Amazingly all his brothers survived, and we talked about how hard it was for his mother to have all five of her sons at war. Then he asked me to follow him into his bedroom so I could see the many photos of his late wife, his children, and grandchildren. He was such a charming and sweet man. He escorted me out of his apartment and down the hall to the elevator and then onto the elevator and into the lobby. He insisted upon walking me all the way to my car, where we said good-bye. Leonide from Belarus is a true gentleman whose mother taught him right.

Leonide lower left and his brothers

Henrietta Herzfeld got her wish, and in October 2014, her first grandchild, Jacob, was born. Jacob's great-great-grandmother is Gitla Libhaber, who survived the Holocaust in Chelm. There were approximately eighteen million Jews worldwide in 1939. After WWII there were about twelve million Jews worldwide. Seventy years later, there are over fourteen million Jews, although the percentage is much lower than prewar, as the number of non-Jews is much higher. In 2013 Jews were 0.02 percent of the world's population. The Nazis tried to eradicate us. Jacob is our victory.

Arlene Blaier Burrows

September 2015

Arlene Blaier Burrows is a clinical psychologist practicing in Williamsville, New York. Formerly, she was on the faculty of SUNY at Buffalo. She has been married to her husband, Ronald, for fifty-two years, and they have three children and six grandchildren. This is her first book.

Printed in the United States
By Bookmasters